From The Pit
To The
Palace

From The Pit To The *Palace*

Patrice Washington

authorHOUSE®

AuthorHouse™
1663 Liberty Drive
Bloomington, IN 47403
www.authorhouse.com
Phone: 1-800-839-8640

Cover design courtesy of Kingdom Dezigns, Dr. LaJaye' Britt
http://www.kingdomdezigns.net/Home.html
Phone: 919-778-7772

Published by AuthorHouse   02/01/2013

ISBN: 978-1-4817-0547-9 (sc)
ISBN: 978-1-4817-0546-2 (e)

Library of Congress Control Number: 2013900445

Any people depicted in stock imagery provided by Thinkstock are models, and such images are being used for illustrative purposes only.
Certain stock imagery © Thinkstock.

This book is printed on acid-free paper.

Contents

FOREWORD

This manuscript is about triumph beyond and above the pain of personal tragedy. It is an autobiography of sorts that brings to the fore a life of trials and trumps. Patrice Washing a daughter, mother, wife and a servant of God who has declared a prophetic calling on her life, presents a sometimes grim but plain view of her life's trials and triumphs. I believe both male and female, that can and do identify with the abuses mentioned here but may not yet identify with the spiritual calling in the subjects life, will see a path to wholeness. They need to know that there is a way of relief, deliverance and yes even recovery from life's most devastating evils, that of abuse and neglect.

The book is about family and decision, choices and influences both negative and positive. The author points to the comfort and pain of familiarity. In one of the chapters, she begins by addressing receiving counsel from ungodly persons. Her focus always keeps you in mind that decisions are indeed a formula for success or failure.

Another very poignant point in this text is the relationship to her grandmother and the last words that she spoke in reference to the author's father. We never know when our last day or words will be lived or spoken, but this woman seemed to have an insight that is rarely seen amongst seasoned folk today. The ability to communicate between the author and this beloved matron will delight you. Sometimes we neglect to realize the importance of confidants, they are repositories of our inner most secrets.

You will see the dynamics of integrated families and how they can affect peace or problems in the family unit. There is much to be said about love and life and the colorful words used to express attitudes and actions will really bring a smile to your face.

There is no way to highlight every significant event in this forward without giving away the truths gleaned from a personal reading. As you inspect the interaction between the real characters herein, you will see the symmetry of the writing in this very personal revelation.

There are just a few points I must present to show you the power of the stories:

- References to abuses in her life and her triumph over them
- Highlighting the significant people in her life that bring the abuse and the healing
- Focus on the faith and spirituality that allow her to deal with the issues faced
- And, an appeal to wholeness through faith and family.

I would be remiss if I did not highlight the focus of the triumph mentioned in the text and that is "personal faith". While I have attempted to bring to you a practical and unbiased presentation of what I have read, I cannot dismiss the work of Christ in the life of this individual. As you will see, there is divine intervention clearly noted from time to time. It is not a surprise that the author wants to testify to the Goodness of her God and His Christ in this eventful life.

If for some reason, you or someone you know is experiencing a life-altering event. And, if you are faced with choices that will bring death to your ability to trust or love. If for some unspoken reason you have been compromised in your heart, violated in your flesh or have lost the promise of a future unscathed by the issues of life, this personal testimony and the triumph of this life will help you to place in perspective the possibilities of hope. Without hope there is despair and death. In this manual, you may find hope for love, hope for healing, hope for deliverance and hope for acceptance. You will see here that spirituality is a formable path for life and restoration. If you scan the words of this document for help or reference, it can be a great resource for you or someone you know. The reader would do well to acquire additional copies to hand out as beacons of light.

Humbly Submitted: Dr. Leon A. Flood Sr. Sacred Th.D.
Grace Point International

Patrice Washington is a woman filled with joy and ambition as well as incredible passion. She walks in the office of Pastor and Prophetess and continues to bless not just the Body of Christ but humanity. She participates in community events and continues to spearhead ministries and programs such as *According To Your Faith Ministries' "Feed My Sheep"*, in which she prepares and serve free food for all who attend. I have personally watched her grow in grace since delivering one of her first sermons and messages at our church.

It was a privilege and honor to have been given the manuscript of this book. As I began to look through it, I immediately concluded that the author had her hand on the pulse of something needed for the church and those who have experienced many traumatic as well as societal issues. From child, mental, physical and emotional abuse, to teenage pregnancy, rape, suicide and being healed, Patrice Washington covers it all. I am sure that everyone who reads or encounters this book will be tremendously blessed and empowered by it. It is a treasure . . . .

Bishop Alfonzo Udell, DD, LHS
Pastor, High Times Christian Fellowship
Presiding Prelate, High Times Christian Fellowship
CEO, Alfonzo Udell Ministries, Inc.
Musical Director, Alfonzo Udell & Chosen
Columbia, South Carolina

In this book, each page will show you that there is a time and a season to everything "Ecclesiastes 3:1". After reading each chapter you will learn that in every thing give thanks for it is the will of God concerning you "1 Thessalonians 5:18".

What you maybe experiencing at this moment may not be designed by God, but His will for you is that you give thanks through it. This mood of thanksgiving will keep you positive and bring you to a perfect end. Jeremiah 29:11 says "I know the thoughts, that I think toward you, saith the Lord, thoughts of peace, and not of evil to give you an expected end". I have observed Pastor Washington experience some of the trials and tribulations that are mentioned in this book and I can attest that she continued to give God praise.

You will also find a rare commodity in this book called transparency between each line and every episode. I feel that it is very important to be transparent and that comes with total honesty. Many people may ask, "Why be so transparent". Well, the only way you can face yourself is that you must be honest and open with one's self. The greatest desire this book represents is that each reader may find total deliverance as you travel "From The Pit To The Palace".

Dr. H. J. Terry Clark
Rehoboth United Assemblies
Perfecting Saints International

Preaching is theologically defined as the spoken communication of divine truth with the view to persuasion. If this definition is true, many preachers do not do this. Too often, God's people sit in the pew to receive an anointed word from the Lord—unfortunately, they end up with a sermon based upon feeling and emotion or something out of a manuscript. The task of being God's messenger is that man live by every Word that proceeds out of the mouth of God.

To the preacher, how can we preach what we do not first believe ourselves? Therefore, our life must go through hard trials that will cause us to rise up a standard of the Word of God against the enemy. Once we have been proven in the area of our ministry God has given to us, then we can release it effectively to God's people. Your faith increases as you obey the voice of God to be led by the Holy Spirit, the people's faith increases by the hearing of the Word and seeing God bring fulfillment to everything that He has promised.

You can be a great bible scholar or a great hooper, saying you have the spirit but by not acting on the Word of God, God will never be revealed in your life. The life of walking in the spirit will open up when you learn how to walk by faith. Do not just say there is anything too hard for God with lip service, believe that if you don't limit God there is no limit to God.

As the Lord, gives the writing of this book to Prophetess Patrice Bell Washington, I pray that the born again believers will be set on fire, to the faith that they need to do the work that God has mandated and designed before he placed you in the womb. I speak blessings in Jesus' name!

~Apostle Phillip O. Coleman, PhD
God's General of Healing
Supernatural Deliverance World Wide Fellowship
Sumter, South Carolina

Greetings I am Dr. LaJaye' Britt, Pastor, Writer, Artist, Husband & Father. I share a deep passion for the art of writing in many different forms.

In the time that I have know Prophetess Washington, the writer & author of this amazing book, it is very clear that she has been through some experiences that could pretentiously have a life changing impact on lives and a greater impact on her readers. Yes, it was no surprise that she would birth a book out of her life's story. In fact just hearing her story I became poised at knowing how much of a reflection of the many things I myself have seen and experienced over my years.

Just the mere mention of the title of this book "From The Pit To The Palace" brings a inter-peace even if in many cases a resolution is not in sight, there is encouragement in this Woman of God story that gives you Hope. She starts by opening her heart and sharing the fortitude of being open and honestly allowing others the ability to gain access to their own freedom from the various hurts of the past, by sharing from the beginning and where it all started. If you have had or experiencing physical, mental or spiritual abuse, Prophetess Writings will become revelatory to your journey of releasing your hurts. I want to encourage every reader to keep reading as I myself have really found hope and a since of peace because as the Bible say we are overcomers by one another's testimonies and in reading this maybe you too will find the tenacity and drive to push forward and birth your next project out of you.

Congratulations Prophetess and we wish you much Success on your endeavor keep writing your best seller is on the way.

Apostle LaJaye' Britt D.Div.

ACKNOWLEDGEMENTS

I would like to first give all the honor and glory to my personal savior Jesus Christ. I thank my husband, James, for sticking with me through some of the hardest points in my life. I would like to thank my children X'Zandrea, Patricia, Praise, and Donte'.

I thank my mother Patricia for loving me when I didn't even love myself and praying for me when I didn't care if I lived or died. I thank God for my father Jerome. I am also thankful to God for all my in-laws who have been closer than my natural family.

I give honor to my Chief Apostle Johnny Clark and Dr. Terry Clark of Perfecting Saints International who accepted me as a daughter and for covering the ministry God placed in my spirit, According To Your Faith Ministry. I am thankful to God for both of them for helping me to stay in God's face with prayer and fasting. I thank them for letting me know that no matter what goes on in my life I have to always keep a praise; and if God said it, it is so!

I truly want to thank my spiritual mother Prophetess Sabrina Brown for taking on the task of loving me through every situation that I have faced and for telling me what thus saith the Lord. I thank her for not compromising and always keeping it real with me.

I thank her for helping me to understand that there has to be a balance in our lives between spiritual and natural things. I thank her for letting me know that always being present in a church building is not being in God's presence. Thank you for allowing God to use you to stir up the gifts of God in my life. I thank you for being the Godly counsel in my life.

I give honor to Apostle Philip O Coleman, who has taught me that there is nothing too hard for God and has caused my faith to soar beyond the mountain tops. He also taught me how to spend my favor and save my money.

Bishop George Bloomer preached a message SEVEN-SEVEN-SEVEN that help put fire under my feet to release this book that I have been sitting on for many years. Demon is defined as an evil spirit, a persistently tormenting person, force, or passion. An example in the dictionary used to define demon is "A man who was finally able to conquer his *demons* and kick his drug habit".

Bishop Bloomer gave an illustration of how a musician can hear a note but can't play it; an artist can see an image but can't paint what he sees. He went on to say all demons don't have to be cast out. Some demons have to be played out, worked out, written out or painted out. I have conquered my demons because God delivered me years ago from a life overflowing in sin but now I am writing them out; to expose them and break every generational curse in Jesus name.

I also want to thank a person I have only met once, but in that one meeting he shared a word with me that will always stick with me through the rest of my life, Bishop Liston Page Jr. He told me to keep balance in my life and to remember that my family is ministry and everything else are assignments.

I thank you for those words more than you know. Those words were life changing and needed during that time in my life. I wanted to support everybody in ministry but forgot that I had a family that needed me just as much.

INTRODUCTION

From The Pit To The Palace is a book based on my life, Prophetess Patrice Washington. In this book it gives an account of the hellish encounters that I have endured but God delivered me out of them all. I was abused from the age of fifteen years old (domestically), raped, abused drugs and alcohol, had mental break downs, became a stripper, sold my body, attempted suicide several times, cutting myself to transfer pain, and the lost of a child.

I was diagnosed with several illnesses I had never even heard of before. Being classified disabled, I delivered a two pound baby at twenty-seven weeks that doctors gave up on but God healed her, my oldest child being taking and incarcerated and then being caught in the state system for two years and then my middle child being arrested for the unthinkable.

A pit in biblical terms refers to hell. A pit is also described as a miserable or depressing place or situation. Many of us have been through several pit situations in our lives. There are many of you who are reading this book who are in a pit right now.

Many people may not understand why I am writing this book, why I am putting all my business out there for the world to view. It is simply because God told me to write the book. I didn't know what the book was supposed to be about in the beginning, all I knew was that God said to write the book.

Even after I got the instructions to write, it took me months before I decided to sit down and try to figure out what I was suppose to say. Eventually after seeking God on this matter he told me to tell my story and to tell all of it. He said don't leave anything out.

Before I became a minister of the gospel God opened many doors for me to share my testimony at women's services and revivals. God sent many confirmations that I was suppose to write a book. There were many prophecies I received about writing a book about my testimonies and how they could see the book being picked up and turned into a movie.

All the prophecies about the book began to vex me so I sat down one night and began to type and before I knew it, the sun was coming up. More days went by and I was stuck in the routine of typing until the sun came up.

I went through a roller coaster of emotions in writing this book. Not because I am not over everything that I endured but because God has been so good to me. He snatched me back from the very fiery pits of hell. So, I have no choice but to totally surrender my life completely to God.

I know there are going to be many people who will be delivered and set free in reading this book, but I also know that there will be many so called Christians who will try to persecute me for my transparency. Everyone has their individual assignment from God. My assignment is to evangelize, be transparent, and to be a tradition breaker.

I believe if people would be concerned about their own assignment from God they wouldn't have to waste time worrying about what avenue another person has taken to get their assignment completed. God uses the foolish to confound the wise.

We can't expect everyone to operate the same exact way. We are a peculiar people. Do not compare yourself to others; just be the very best you that God has called you to be.

We all go through changes. One of my favorite preachers made a statement about change. He said "Nothing welcomes change except a wet baby". We as adults fight against change no matter how bad our lives are. We need change but, a baby got more sense to cry out when they need to be changed.

I realized that I needed change in my life and I cried out to God to get me out of the stinking mess that I had allowed myself to get in. I thank God that he heard my cry and answered me. I am the type of person when I say the words I know, I understand, I have been there and done that. I am not just talking, it is the truth.

As you read this book you will find that you are not alone. Someone else has encountered some of the same things you have dealt with or are dealing with right now. I want you to know that you will make it. Satan has already been defeated. Stand still and let God fight your battles because our names are victory.

Know that God will not put more on you than you can handle, he will always provide a way of escape to those who are willing and obedient to him. Maybe you say you haven't been obedient and willing so you feel like you have no escape, all you have to do is repent and strive to do better.

God will forgive you and provide you a way of escape. Know that all things really do work together for your good!!! Now let's take the ride of your life "From The Pit To The Palace".

ABUSE STARTS AT A YOUNG AGE

My family lived up north for many years. My Dad went in the Army after high school. I was born on the army base. I was told that there was a lot of arguing between my mother and my father and it eventually it turned physical.

My dad was arrested while in the Army. The authorities found many pounds of marijuana in his possession. They told my mother that she had a couple of hours to get out of the state and she wasn't welcome back.

This wasn't an isolated incident concerning my father, he was in the papers and arrested for several crazy things he did. I read an article where they said my dad held people hostage in a parking lot with a gun. They later found out that it was a toy gun.

He also was in the papers because he ran in a house fire to save some kids after the fire fighters told him not to and the city took him to court for disobeying a direct ordered. He did save some of the kids out of the fire.

Being in the military caused my father to be a very strong minded man but he also had a lot of anger issues. People in the military see a lot of things that most people couldn't handle.

They see their friends get killed while in war as well as experience the after effects of killing people. It is hard for people to cope once they get out of the military. Some people, like my dad, have anger issues, nightmares, and vivid dreams. It does not give them an excuse for their actions but, it gives you a better understanding why they act the way they do.

A lot of people that have been in the military seek help but they can't find it. The government thinks because they give them a check that they have are taking care of the soldiers but many soldiers turn to drugs and alcohol to try to forget what they have been through or numb the pain they feel inside. It is also hard for them to open up to people because it is only so much they can share as they have an oath that has to be upheld. I have done much research and found that domestic abuse is highest in people who are in the military or have been in the military at some point in their lives.

There are different types of abuse. I would like to take the time to discuss the types of abuse that I personally have endured. The three types of abuse I want to talk about are mental, physical, and spiritual abuse. I know everyone can relate to physical abuse in some way, whether it was you, family or friends that has encountered it.

Physical abuse is any act resulting in a non-accidental physical injury; including not only intentional assault but also the results of unreasonable punishment. It is when you allow someone to push, slap, kick, bite or punch you. It all is abuse.

Mental abuse is when there is a consistent and chronic pattern of maltreatment that is causing significant distress. It's when you allow someone to tell you that you are not worth anything, no one else will want you, you are ugly, and you will never be anything.

Spiritual Abuse is when you allow someone to use their authority to satisfy their own needs at the expense of you. It is the mistreatment of others, where power is used to bolster the position or needs of a leader, without regard for others' well-being or spiritual empowerment.

I want you to notice that I said (you) before each explanation because these are things that you allow. We allow people to do these things to us and our God. You may ask "Why did she say we allow them to do these things to our God"? It is because God dwells in us and our body is his temple. God said he has not given us a spirit of fear. The reason we allow people to abuse us is because we fear everything that they have told us is true or we fear the abuser themselves.

Fear is false evidence appearing real. The devil is a liar and everything he has told us up until this point I bind it up and send it back to the pits of hell in Jesus name. I cover everyone's mind that read this book and cast out every imagination that would try to exalt itself against the will of God for your life. God has not given you the spirit of fear; he has given you love, power and a sound mind. You will not go crazy, you will not kill yourself but you will be made whole. You are not alone. Seek help now.

All the devil need is a little room to ease his way in. We have to stop giving the devil permission to come in by allowing people to take total control over our lives. God said we are the head and not the tail, above and not beneath, the lender and not borrower. Let's start acting like it.

DIVINE CONNECTION

My mom and I moved down south when I was four. We moved to a small country town with my great-grandmother. My great-grandmother was a very strong woman who loved God. My great-grandfather died years before we moved there. She loved hard and she also punished hard. I grew up in the era when if you got in trouble everybody in the neighborhood was going to punish you. You had to go and get your own switch and if you brought a thin one back, you were made to go get several more and they would braid them together and cut your butt.

We attended a small Baptist church there. We were always in church. I learned about God at an early age. I can remember even at a young age having dreams and they would come true. I was too young to understand what was going on then. I grew up around older people so that cause me to be a little more mature than most kids my age.

My great-grandmother had a garden and huge apple tree in her back yard. I enjoyed helping her in the garden. I was just terrified of the garden snakes. No matter how much my great-grandmother said they wouldn't harm me, when I ran across one it would be running one way and I was running another way.

My mom met a man and they started dating. He was the father that I didn't have. He took care of me and his family became closer to me than my blood family. We moved to the city when I started first grade. I never had many friends so I stayed to myself most of the time. My mom use to work all the time. She worked at fast-food restaurants and hotels during the day and at a bingo hall at night. When she wasn't working at bingo she was playing bingo. She would take me to work with her sometimes but people complained about me being too young to be there with her. I believe it had nothing to do with my age, they were just jealous because I was always winning. So my mom had to find someone to keep me while she worked at night.

My mother asked a neighbor if she could watch me. My mom didn't know that this was a divine connection. Our neighbor who began to watch me had a husband and two children. Our neighbor's husband was a Pastor in the Apostolic Faith Ministry. Her husband became my god-father and her kids were not just my friends but, my sister and brother.

We were in church all the time. I loved it because they did things at their church I had never seen before in my life. I remember seeing someone shout and speak in tongues for the first time. Being kids we would pick and imitate the people we saw in church as most kids do. My god-father was a force to be reckoned with. He was anointed to preach, teach, prophecy, sing, play many instruments, heal the sick, and cast out demons.

It may not seem like that's nothing to you but to a child that had never seen people who operated in the anointing it was much. I called him the miracle worker for two reasons, one because he use to always sing that song and two because he really was a miracle worker.

My god-father and I became so close to the point that I was closer to him than anyone in my life including my own mother and step-father. I use to joke and call him Beast and The God Father because his favorite movies were Beauty and The Beast and The God Father. He said that he was the beast and his wife was the beauty and that there was no god-father greater than him, so he was The God-Father.

Over the years my god-father adopted other girls as his god-daughters. He was kind of hard on my other god sisters. I was one of the ones who wasn't saved or had received the gift of the Holy Ghost. Well I didn't know then, but I know now that I was saved.

I actually got saved at a community Girl Scout meeting ran by a group of white Christians. In Romans 10:9-10 it tells you how to be saved. I knew who God was, confessed with my mouth, asked for forgiveness of my sins, believed he died for my sins, and that he raised from the dead. That's being saved. I just wasn't wholly sanctified.

TRYING TO FIT IN

At the age of twelve years old I went to work with my mom to a bingo hall. They had not opened yet as we got there early so I went in the bathroom and as I was leaving out I saw an Angel. It was tall, with a white flowing gown, and it had a glow around it. I was so terrified, I ran out the bathroom crying.

When I got home I told my god-father about it and he told me that I had a gift and that there was no need for me to be scared. He told me that I had a zeal for Jesus and that God had a work for me to do in the kingdom. I was crying at this time, I told him that I didn't want the gift.

He prayed a prayer that God would allow my gifts to lay dormant until I was equipped to operate in them. I didn't see anything else after his prayer.

Also at the age of twelve years old I had my first boyfriend, we dated for two years. He would always want to argue and fight. He would break up with me just so he could mess with other girls and then he would come back to me.

I never kissed or did anything else with him and I knew that's why he kept breaking up with me. He was horrible to me, but because he was popular I felt like I was blessed that he wanted to be with me, I put up with it. I didn't have friends to talk to because all the girls hated me and picked on me. I had to bottle a lot of things up.

I was terrified of him. He was a bully; even a lot of the guys wouldn't step to him. I had one guy that was a class clown that I would talk to at times and he helped me build up my self-confidence.

I finally got enough strength to break up with him for good. He attacked me on the school bus and ripped my earring out my ear, this was the first and last time he hit me. I fought back.

Today I wear the reminder of how my abuse started at a young age. My hole in my ear is still torn. I started to date a guy I really liked he was on the basketball team and I was a cheerleader. He was actually the first boy I ever kissed one night coming back from a game. Then rumors spread that I couldn't kiss. It crushed me and killed any confidence I had in myself. The issue got worst because as I stated the girls hated me but the boys were noticing me so I gravitated to the boys.

I wasn't sexually active like other girls that were in school with me. There was a girl in sixth grade that had a baby. When I turned fourteen I noticed that the one girl I considered to be my friend was having sex so I felt like I should do it to fit in. She told me how great it was but she never told me that's why she stayed depressed. She was depressed a lot because the guys she was sleeping with wanted her for that reason only.

The summer before high school I turned fifteen, that's when I decided to have sex. It was honestly one of the worst experiences I have ever had in my life. The guy struggled and finally he asked me was it my first time and I said yes and he fussed at me for not telling him. I actually felt so embarrassed. After my first experience I felt like I had done something. I thought I was grown.

A couple weeks later I went to the skating rink where I met a guy. We were watching each other but we never approached one another. Before I left I gave him my phone number. We started dating. I had no idea what was in store for me. We begin to have sex. My god-father noticed the change in me immediately. He actually went and bought me some condoms and told me that I needed to be careful. I denied to him that I was having sex.

When we sin and are disobedient to God we alter our life but our purpose has to be fulfilled. You know we can't always do the same thing that everybody else does and get the same result when we have a call on our lives. God chastens those he loves.

My family didn't approve of us dating because he was a little older. He was street smart and taught me a lot, mostly bad things. I lived a sheltered life before I met him but he exposed me to drug dealers, robbing, and a lot of other unlawful things. The more people talk against us dating the closer we became. We helped each other get through issues we were dealing with. He had lost his brother, whom was killed over a girl. I believe to this day that is why he has no respect or regard for women.

Parents have to be careful of the tactics they use to make a point to their children. We mean good but if we do or say the wrong things or the right thing at the wrong time, it could push the children in the direction we do not want them to go in. The Bible states we must be wise as serpents, and harmless as doves.

FINDING OUT I WAS PREGNANT

I went through so many things while dating him. The mental abuse was extreme. I tried to leave several times but I felt like he actually possessed my soul. I did not want to stay with him but I felt like I could not leave.

During one of the times when I broke up with him he called my mom and told her I was pregnant. My mom came to me and asked me about it and I told her no. I told her no, not because I was trying to hide it but, I really didn't know. I hadn't missed my menstrual cycle, so how was I supposed to know.

I will never forget that day. My mom took me to the health department. I was wearing some short shorts because I had actually started losing weight. I just knew I wasn't pregnant. The nurse came in and did the test. She came back in shortly and told me that the test was positive. The nurse asks me if I wanted her to tell my mom. Of course, the answer was yes.

My mother flipped out right there in the office. She told me I wasn't having a baby and that I had to get rid of it. She said I was still a baby. She went on and on and on. I was scared to even get in the car to even go home with her. I just knew she was going to kill me. By the time night came everybody and their momma knew I was pregnant.

When I got home I called my boyfriend and told him that I was pregnant and he was happy. I don't know if he was happy because I was pregnant or because he found a way to make me stay with him but one thing that I did know was that I was scared!

I was fifteen years old and pregnant. My mother was livid at me and most of my family and the other adults that found out talked junk about me. They didn't talk about me behind my back they said it to my face. I did not have anyone to talk to. All of the negativity thrust me back closer to my child's father who was abusing me even the more now.

It seemed as though my pregnancy caused the abuse to intensify. It went from mental to extreme physical abuse. I was told I was fat and ugly, nobody else would want me and I was not allowed to have any friends.

I remember one night he called and told me that he was going to kill me when I went to the bus stop the next morning for breaking up with him. So I got up early in the morning and tried to walk to school before he got up. As I got about one mile from the school he came running up behind me and started to beat me down to the ground. I was five months pregnant at this time.

He told me if he could not have me no one else would. We were in front of this house and a man ran outside and told him to get off me. He asked him what his problem was, and told him that men don't hit on women. My child's father took off running.

The man called the police and drove me to the school. An ambulance came and I went to the hospital and I had suffered damage to my ear drum from the blows. Because of the injury I endured to my head, I couldn't hear out my ear for a long period of time. He later went to jail and he stayed in jail throughout out my pregnancy.

I had a beautiful little girl and that's when I realized I was still a child but now I had the responsibilities of an adult. My daughter's father got out of jail a couple of months after her birth.

He came to visit her and seemed to have changed. We started back dating. I thought that it would be best for my daughter and for me to stay with her father. Besides, my mother and his mother had left our fathers and we wanted better for our child. After a while the aggression started back up again.

PICKED ON BY THE CHURCH

Some people in the church had a problem with my pregnancy. Because of the things that was said and the way that people made me feel, it made me want to never go to church again. It's degradation when you dread going to the house of God. My god father told me I didn't have to answer to them and not to worry about them talking about me. He said "they talked about Jesus". People were trying to figure out how I could have gotten pregnant being under such a mighty man of God.

People in the church see you do something wrong and they tell you that your not saved or you are going to hell. They act like they haven't done anything wrong. At some point in everybody's life they had to go to God for forgiveness for something. All have sinned. People get so caught up on the sin they can see but there are many people who are sinning and we would never know unless they told us, or we were actually there during the act, or if God chooses to expose them.

If someone has made you feel like the mistake you have made is beyond correction, know that everybody makes mistakes and Jesus is the ultimate white out. Know that if you have asked for forgiveness, God has forgiven you and has made you white as snow. Move on. Stop dwelling on the past because the past has passed.

There is a difference between being saved, sanctified, Holy Ghost filled, and a person who just go to church. A lot of people just go to church! They go to church to please other people, to be seen, to say that they are a member of so and so church, to see who they can mate up with, to find out the newest gossip or to get a temporarily emotional high.

These are the people that you need to beware of. They are people who have a form of Godliness but deny the true undenying power of God. They are also considered to be the counsel of the ungodly. They say but don't do.

When you accept Jesus as your personal savior, ask to be forgiven and began to turn from sin you are saved. As you renounce sin and present your body to God as a living sacrifice you are being sanctified. When the

Holy Ghost comes it becomes your comfort, your guide, and it gives you power to resist the devil and he must flee.

One of the major things I believe a lot of people need to be delivered from is people. I personally had to go on a thirty day fast to defeat this myself. Ask God to give you power to be delivered from people and what they think or say about you and he will do it.

WORSHIP NO OTHER

My Godfather was a very powerful man. I saw people get saved, receive the Holy Ghost, be healed and have demons cast out of them. Many people looked up to him. I felt that it got to a point where people stopped searching for God for themselves and only responded off of every word my God-father spoke.

I felt like some people worshiped him instead of just the God in him. Many people still operate like this. They never read the Bible for themselves; they only know what the preacher preaches. They never pray for themselves but always want somebody to pray for them. Never get to the point where you put all trust in man and not seek God for yourself as that is a form of worship.

In 1995 my God-father got sick and the doctors didn't think he would make it. He was very ill but, he survived. He got out of the hospital and he preached a sermon "Like Father like Son". I will never forget this because this is the last time he ever preached.

In that sermon my God-father talked about how Jesus died and he rose on the third day. He preached about how he was sick and they said he wouldn't make it but on the third day he woke up. It was a great sermon.

A couple of days later he called me and said that he was getting his car serviced and he needed to spend time with me. He said he was coming to pick me up after they were finished with the car.

I waited but, he never showed up. My daughter's father had come by to visit while I waited and finally I got a knock on the door and it was my God-father's sister in law. I was upstairs so I open the window and she said "Pastor has passed". I asked her what she was talking about. She yelled "Pastor has passed".

I told her she didn't know what she was talking about because I had just spoken with him and he was on the way to get me. She repeated herself Pastor has passed and she left. I called my mom screaming and crying and she had no idea what I was saying, so she came home. I told her what happened. She didn't believe it so she called to find out for herself.

When she confirmed what had been told to me. I actually felt like I had died.

I loved my God-father more than almost anything in the world at that time in my life. I ran out the door and ran until I couldn't run any more. I collapsed on the ground and it was pouring down raining. My mom found me down the street on the ground in the rain screaming and crying. I was so numb.

I refused to believe that he was dead. I can remember thinking they were going to call and say he's alive. I refused to believe my God-father with that much anointing and power was gone. I can remember sitting at the funeral saying over and over again in my spirit "Get up!" He never moved.

It did not set in to me that he was really gone until they closed the casket. As they closed the casket it felt like a piece of my heart was ripped right out of my chest. My dad, rock, instructor, friend, teacher, and counselor was gone. My God-father church was independent so when he died our church went through many transitions. The people that remained together joined another church as a whole.

RECEIVING THE HOLY SPIRIT

One day I was sitting downstairs in our apartment. That day I was really missing my God-father. I put one of his tapes in. While crying, I begin to sing along and doing what he was singing on the tape. He sung "Clap your hands, stomp your feet, jump up and down, turn around, and praise the Lord". On the third time of me doing this as I turned around I couldn't stop.

It felt like a very cold harsh wind was blowing through the whole apartment. When I finally stopped I fell to the floor and opened my eyes and begin to speak in tongues. I was scared and excited all at the same time.

I called my God-mother and asked her how you know if you received the Holy Ghost. She asked me did I think I had received the Holy Ghost. I told her I didn't know but, something happened that had never happened before. She said she couldn't tell me. I had to know for myself. I told her what happened but she never confirmed to me that I had received the gift of the Holy Ghost. I was confused. I thought to myself why she wouldn't tell me that I had received the Holy Ghost. So I thought maybe I didn't have it.

Everybody else I knew that received the Holy Ghost had received it by tarrying at the altar. We were a very traditional church. We didn't wear pants, earrings, or make up. It was a very strict Pentecostal-Holiness church.

We went to church that night. The Pastor ask me to stand up before he began to teach Bible study and he said "I heard that you think you received the Holy Ghost". I said "Yes Sir". He asks me how I knew if I had received the Holy Ghost. I didn't know what to say so I didn't answer him so he continued with Bible study.

Then he came back to me again and asked the same questions. I wanted to say something but, I didn't know what to say. Again I remained silent. He went back into Bible study. When it got close to the end of Bible study he asked me again and I said to myself God please give me the right answer because I know what I experienced. Immediately I began to shake and cry and when I open my mouth I started to speak in tongues. He said she got it and everyone began to rejoice. We might not have the right words to say but, God will speak for us. He said it will flow out of our bellies like rivers of living water.

I continued to deal with my child's father because I wanted her to have him in her life. Sometimes we make decisions that we think is for the best but it turns out to be the worst. He continued to abuse me and he was also cheating on me.

I finally made up in my mind that I was worth more than how he was treating me. I attempted to break up with him for the last time because I realized that it was not benefiting my daughter by her father being there. Staying with him was teaching her that it was okay for a man to mistreat and abuse a woman. After we finished arguing on the phone, he threatened to kill me once again. I hung up the phone and went to church for a Thanksgiving program.

While we were having service my daughter's father came to the church and said openly he was going to kill me. I believed he meant it that time because he actually came to the church with a gun.

The church began to go into warfare in the spirit. The Pastor took me to the back in his office and told me that if I had any family members out of town that I needed to leave because if I didn't my family would be burying me.

My mom arranged for me to go up north with my grandmother. The day after I arrived at my paternal grandparents' house my mom called me. She told me that she had some bad news to tell me. I knew it had to be real bad because she was scared to tell me.

She told me that my Pastor was preaching a Sermon called "It's Finish" that morning and he walked over to someone in the church and died right there, in church. I was devastated. This was the second Pastor I had lost within a six month period.

DOUBT KICKED IN

I felt like some kind of way it was my fault that people close to me were dying. My God-father had gone into warfare on my behalf because I had found my daughter's father was cheating and the young lady he cheated with was HIV positive. I just knew he had given it to me. My God-father called me and told me God said he blocked it and that my tests would be negative and they were. Praise God.

Then months later my new Pastor was praying for me so that my daughter's father didn't find me and kill me and after he sent me away, he died. I really began to believe that it was my fault that people were dying.

The devil will make you feel bad about stuff you have no control over. The devil wants to control our thoughts because where our thoughts are our body will follow. I want to stop here and encourage someone to let them know that it is not your fault. God has a set time and season for things to occur. Some things occurred because others stepped out of the will of God.

It seems like the events you are enduring are because of something you did but I pray now that God will destroy the spirit of condemnation, self-accusation, self-rejection, oppression, depression, double mindedness, judgment, and deception in the name of Jesus. I pray that the peace that surpass all understanding will fill your very mind, body, and soul and I command your thoughts to line up with the will of God for your life, in Jesus name!!!

When I finally came back home things were different. There was heaviness in the atmosphere. I left excited about God and came back angry at God. I started to doubt God and I got to a point that I didn't even care.

I continued to go to church and sung on the choir but I did it out of obligation not because I wanted to. There are so many people today that are doing things out of obligation and God isn't getting any glory out of it. When we do things out of obligation there is no anointing, no power, and no satisfaction to God.

Instead of you building ministry you are demolishing it. Don't quit on your God given assignment. Do not be weary in well doing, you will reap if you faint not. If this is you, pray that God will restore the zeal to complete what he has started in you.

I ran into an older guy I went to school with one night at the bowling alley. He was older than me so when he showed an interest in me I was excited. He was the type of guy that many of the girls ran after.

We were together a couple of months and this turned out to be another intimidating relationship. This relationship was more sexual than anything else. We used condoms all the time but one night he didn't have one. I told him no because I did not want to get pregnant but, it happened anyway.

Some people would have considered this date rape but I did not view it that way. I felt like it was not the fact that I did not want to have sex, it was the fact that he did not have protection. We broke up after this incident and things were never the same between us again.

PREGNANT AGAIN

Immediately I began to get sick and I found out that I was pregnant about four weeks later. Of course he did like most young boys do. He denied that it was his.

After my daughter was born I actually decided to search for him to make him pay. I went to a club one night and ran into his brother and he got me back in contact with her father.

He never stepped up to the plate but his mother and siblings helped me so much. We finally went to take a paternity test and it read in modern day terms "YOU ARE THE FATHER".

After the birth of my second daughter the church made me sit in the back of the church, get off the choir and told me I had to go before the church and ask for forgiveness. I left that church. I felt like the only person I had to ask for forgiveness from was God. I graduated from high school months earlier. I had been working ever since I had my first daughter in ninth grade. I was told I wouldn't be able to complete school and I wouldn't ever have anything, so I had to prove everyone wrong.

I went to regular school during the day, adult school at night to make up the credits I was lacking to graduate with my class, and went to work at a fast food restaurant after night school and closed five to six nights a week. Guess what, I did it. I graduated with my class.

FREEDOM AT LAST

My mom and I were bumping heads. She told me what many youth have heard throughout the years, if I thought I was grown then I needed to get my own place. I guess I thought I was grown because I moved out and got my own apartment. I didn't move in with anybody else, I went out and got my own.

When I moved into my own place I had so much freedom. An idle mind is the devil's workshop. I had too much time and freedom on my hands, so I would find anything to fill it. I attracted a new group of friends. When all your friends stay at home with their parents but they have you, someone that has their own place, you will find out they are not really your friends at all but are using you as a scapegoat. Once I realized this and I was getting cussed out by parents for their kids hanging out, I started hanging out with some friends from work that were older than me.

We practically lived in the club. Every time the doors would open we were there and we stayed there until it closed. We had a schedule. There was a club for every single day of the week.

For me I didn't look at the club as just a hook up spot like the other girls that I went out with, I really loved to dance. As many of you already know you can't be in club environments as long as we were, and not end up doing drugs or drinking alcohol. I was actually introduced to weed by the manager on my job at the time.

At the time, I felt like I did not have a care in the world, like my problems just faded away. It was just a temporary fix but for a brief moment while I was high, I didn't have to think about anything. I thought I was free but as the high settled I still had the worries about bills, past issues, and my kids because they were acting up. I rapidly became what most people would call a weed head. I only dated drug dealers because I thought I was getting something for free but I know now, nothing in this world is free. I endured all types of abuse just to get a fix and to be, what I thought, being spoiled by men.

One day this guy came on my job and I asked him about some weed, he looked like he was high. He said he had some. So the next day I made plans to go and hang out with him. When I went to meet him, he took me back to a hotel room. We smoked and I began to feel funny. I fell back on the bed and laid there and looked at the ceiling. It seemed as if I was watching a movie slide show. I couldn't move. Then I saw the door open and another guy came in. The guy that I went to chill with began to take advantage of me. I didn't have any control of my body. I couldn't even speak. I can remember trying to speak but every word was slurred and unrecognizable.

I blacked out. I found out later that the weed had been laced with embalming fluid. My body felt the effects of that laced weed for about two months. I felt so stupid. I know you are thinking "I know she never smoked again", wrong I did, even more.

THE WRECK

After that I was always so agitated. I know my mom knew something was going on with me but she never put her finger on it. I decided I was going to take my daughter to her dad because I got mad at my mom. My mother refused to watch my daughter so that I could go to work and then to the club afterward. So jumped in my new car and decided that I was going to drive over seven hours one way by myself. I didn't tell any one I was going except the guy I was dating at the time. I tried to get him to ride with me but he declined.

When I finally made it, it was late. My daughter's grandmother told me to stay and try to get some sleep. I told her no. All I was thinking in my mind was, I refuse to stay in a house with my daughter's father and his other baby momma, who had a child right after I had my daughter.

I jumped in my car mad at the world and started to drive back down the road. I got tired so I pulled over on an exit ramp and went to sleep in the car behind an eighteen-wheeler that had also pulled over.

I slept for about two hours. The sun was coming up so I begin to drive again. It seemed like as soon as I started driving a real heavy sleep fell on me. I fell asleep driving. I heard a man voice say "Wake up". There was no one in the car with me but when I open my eyes I saw flowers and trees coming toward me. I had run off an embankment. The car stopped when I hit a tree. I tried to open the door but it was jammed. I sat there for a moment in a daze. As I looked out the cracked windshield I noticed that the car was on fire.

I was trapped! I had to lift the dashboard off my legs to climb out of the front seat to the back of the car. I kicked the back door open, to get out because it was also stuck. I then had to climb up the hill to get to the interstate away from my burning car.

When I got to the top of the hill it started to drizzle. There was a man that pulled up and said that he saw me swerving in his rear view mirror and when he looked again I was gone, I had ran off the road. He was trying to explain how he had to drive to the nearest exit to turn around to get back to help me and that he had called 911. He said "Help is on the way"!

I was in shock. It all had not set in yet but after a few minutes I collapsed. The paramedics got there and revived me waving ammonium carbonate in my face. When I got to the hospital they asked me for emergency contact. I told them to call my mom.

When my mom found out she was upset but also shocked because she had no idea that I had left the state. She had to drive six hours to come get me. She went to the junk yard first to get my stuff out the car.

When she got there one of the workers told her that who ever was in that car was blessed to be alive. My mom ended up getting lost and it ended up taking her a whole lot longer to pick me up from the hospital.

On the ride home my mom was playing a song called "Second Chance". I cried because I knew God had given me another chance in life. I knew I should have died in that car wreck. I had to wear a brace on my leg from my ankle all the way up to my hip for a long time and I had to go and get fluid drained off my knee weekly.

It seems like I would have given my all to God after that but I didn't. I continued to live my life the way I wanted to. I was still drinking, smoking, and going to the club. I gave God time when I wanted to. Usually it was on Tuesday for Bible study, Thursday for intercessory prayer and Sunday for regular church services.

I know you are probably thinking how in the world did she live life "in the world" and continue to go to church that often. The answer to that question is the same way that some of you are still doing right now. The one thing about me is I never tried to hide anything up until this point that I did, and neither did I turn my back completely on God. Some people may not understand it and some may say that I was double minded which would have been a true statement but I couldn't let go of my faith. It was the only thing that kept me alive.

THE ABORTION

When I got home after the car wreck I found out I was pregnant again. I was on my third child and I was not one hundred percent sure who the father was. I had a good idea but I was not sure.

I was messing around with one of my ex-boyfriends as well as a dealer that I had met one night when we went to get breakfast after leaving the club. He was with his brother and they had some of the finest cars you ever seen.

My ex was my ex for a reason. I did not know how the dealer would take the news of my pregnancy especially since we were not in a serious relationship and I did think that the he wanted to settle down. I told both of them that I was pregnant and that it was a toss up to which one was the father.

Neither one of them was mad but I did not see where either one of them would step up to the plate. I made a decision that I would not take care of another child alone. I decided to have an abortion.

I was almost four months when I got the money together to have the abortion. I had to go out of state to get the abortion because there were no upcoming appointments in my state. My mom and my grandmother took me to North Carolina to have the procedure done.

All I could think about on my way there was that my God-father would be so upset with me, even though he had passed. I knew it was wrong but, I knew I couldn't take care of the baby on my own.

Do I think I made the right decision? No, but at the time I felt like I didn't have any other option. I had other options, but no one took the time to minister to me to tell me what those options were. All people did was criticize me. For anyone who is in this situation I encourage you to reach out for help. If you know anyone who is going through this, please help them. Give them resources that can help them make a better decision than I did. You can contact your local health department and they can give you other options other than an abortion.

When I arrived to the clinic they required that you get an ultrasound. They said it was to verify how far along I was. I started to have second thoughts but I went ahead and had the procedure done. It was the worst pain I ever experienced in my life.

The nurse had me sit in a room with all the other girls that just had the same procedure done. I got sick. I started to vomit and cramp real bad. The nurse told me, after the fact, that I should not have eaten anything prior to the procedure. I had to stay longer than the other girls but, finally they let me leave.

A couple of days later I went to the club with some friends. They felt that I really needed to get out the house. The first thing I did when I got to the club was get a drink and go straight to the dance floor. I was dancing, having a ball, when all of a sudden I got nausea and started cramping extremely bad. I felt like I had urinated on myself but when I went to the restroom I noticed that I was hemorrhaging. I had big clots of tissue coming out of me. I was terrified and I surely thought I was about to bleed to death. I was rushed to the hospital.

As I was on the way to the hospital I began to pray and to tell God that I shall not die but live, after all it was in His word and I knew he couldn't lie. I know your sitting there thinking that I had no right using the word of God because I had an abortion and then had the nerves to go to the club. Oh you hypocrites. It's plenty of things you have done and you knew it was wrong and as soon as you got in trouble, who did you call on? Perhaps it was God.

I remember my God-father telling me that I had life or death in my mouth and what so ever I say; I can have it, only if I believed. So I spoke life. I also remember him telling me that Jesus came for the sinner. At that point I felt like I was the one lost sheep that had strayed away from the ninety-nine. I knew I was wrong for what I did so I asked God to forgive me for my sins and I also made a vow that I would never have another abortion in my life. I also promised if ever the opportunities arise, I would like to be used to talk to females to encourage them not to allow abortion be their only and final option.

The doctor finally came in and I had to explain to the doctor that I just had an abortion. First thing I noticed was that the doctor didn't seem shocked. He said "I see this all the time after this kind of procedure, if not done right". The way he talk to me, if I didn't know better, would have made me think that there was nothing wrong with me having the abortion. He made it seem like it was a normal thing.

There are a lot of preachers today who don't preach against sin any more. They do not teach that holiness is a lifestyle. They make it seem like its okay to sin as long as you show up to church.

They make it seem like its okay as long as you singing on the choir and serve on all the auxiliaries you serve on. No sin is okay and it is not okay for us to make it seem like it is okay!!!

The doctor told me that the doctor who did the abortion didn't scrape my cervix and that I had a lot of tissue (after birth) that was still in me. I had to get a DNC; they scrapped my cervix and gave me antibiotics to take so that I didn't develop an infection. I was discharged the next day.

I went home. I tried to rest but I couldn't. I felt so condemned and very depressed about the abortion. I got so depressed. I felt like I wanted to die because I viewed myself as a murder. The depression got so bad I had to be hospitalized for it. I stayed there for a week.

When I got home I tried to act like everything was alright but it was not. I still felt depressed and condemned. Some of my so called friends at the time came over and convinced me that I needed to get out of the house because I was shutting everyone out my life. I have learned that as we go through trials and tribulations in our life if we do not cast down the imaginations, the thoughts, which the devil bring to us we will find ourselves isolating ourselves from everybody and everything. Unrepented sin will cause us to even separate ourselves from God.

Unrepented sin makes you feel like you are not worthy of even God's love. You have to keep yourself surrounded with real men and women of God with good character to keep you encouraged because some times, the hardest thing to do is to encourage yourself.

IT COULD HAVE BEEN ME

I allowed myself to be encouraged and counseled by unsaved people who really didn't have my best interest in mind. The Bible refers to it as the counsel of the ungodly. I realized the majority of the time those friends just needed me out the house to drive them where they needed to go. A couple of weeks later a few of us went to the same club I was rushed out of weeks earlier. I was on the stage dancing with this guy. Then all of a sudden there was a big fight that broke out and the bouncers started throwing a whole bunch of guys out of the club.

After everything calmed down they cut the music back on and everybody started back dancing again. The club was packed to capacity. In just a short while later, a couple of the guys that got kicked out came back in the club shooting. They did not care who got shot. Everybody was running and screaming. I fell backwards and the guy I was dancing with fell on top of me. He kept yelling "I got hit". I didn't understand what he meant but he had got shot. All of us can look back over our life and realize that God has blocked something that could have happen to us.

Something could have caused us to be dead today but, God blocked it. All I could think about that night when we left the club was that could have been me!

As always, my friends and I would say we were not going back to the club, when we encountered fights or shootings but every weekend we would be right back at the club. Not a different club but the same club. Even in our stupidity and disobedience God still protects us.

A couple weeks later we went to another club in a really bad neighborhood and a fight broke out. I ran out the club to get in my car but on the way to my car I ran into the guy who was fighting.

He was headed back to the club with a gun in his hand. He told me "If I wanted to live I better get in my car". I ran as fast as I could and jumped in my car, locked the door, and slumped all the way under my dashboard. As soon as I locked the door I heard gun shots. The other girls that were riding with me were locked out the car banging on the door, trying to get me to open it. I finally opened the door for them and we left. This is just another case of God's favor and protection over my life.

Almost every relationship I was in was very abusive; that is if you would even call it a relationship. Some of the guys I dated had girlfriends. I even dated a guy for almost ten years before his girlfriend found out that he was messing with me. We still talked after the blow up. Of course, he eventually broke it off with me, even though he said he cared about me so much.

One thing I realized was I wasn't his girlfriend. I was the girl on the side. His family and friends all knew about me but, in the end, none of that mattered.

For the man or woman that feels as though it doesn't matter as long as they are there for you and/or they take care of you, you know deep down inside you want the whole woman or man not apart of them. Why be second best when you can be the best. It's time to let go, move on, and make room for the man or woman that God has prepared just for you.

I always found myself involved with men who were financially stable. The majority of them were drug dealers. I was given pretty much what ever I wanted. I thought I was happy and on top of the world. I was given what appeared to be free drinks, weed, money, and trips.

I shopped so much that I would buy clothes so I didn't have to wash me and my children's clothes. I was the one to round up all her friends to go to the club and tell everyone with me I would pay their way in the club and drinks were on me. They just didn't know the physical and mental abuse I had to endure to get the money I had. The devil will make things convenient for you to keep you out of the will of God.

MY FATHER

My paternal grandmother and my great-grandmother were like my best friends. My grand mother lived up north and she had been fussing at me about the relationship that I had with my father for a while. I wanted nothing to do with him. You have to remember that my father didn't raise me.

My mom's boyfriend and my godfather raised me. Around the age of twelve my father drove down with some of his friends to get me for the first time. I can remember them drinking and smoking the whole trip back up north. This is when I found out that my father had a serious substance abuse problem and that he was in and out of jail a lot. No one talked negatively about my father to me I came to my conclusions about him by what I experienced while I was in his care.

There are very few times I can remember being around my father and he was sober. He always did a lot of cursing. During my visit with my father, he took me to meet a couple of family members and then I was left with a woman I did not know. I understand that it was his girlfriend, but I did not leave my mother to spend time with his girlfriend.

He promised me that he was going to take me to a theme park. It never happened. He didn't come home that day and when he did come home he said he had gotten robbed. My father always had an excuse for why he couldn't do what he promised me he would do. It wasn't just excuses, it was straight lies. The scary part is that I believe sometimes he believed his own lies.

As I got older I found out how he abused my mother and how he was addicted to crack, marijuana, and alcohol. He was a functioning addict and you only knew it if he let his guard down. I said to myself what most children say when they have parents or close loved ones that have addictions "I will never drink or smoke". One thing that I have learned, we can say many things from our mouth but we really don't know what we will do until we are faced with life's problems.

I now know that there was a generational curse of addiction that went back generations on both sides of my family that needed to be broken. You do not have to be a product of your environment. You do not even have to do what your parents did or even act like them for that matter. Once you come to God behold all things are made new.

GRANDMA

My father's mother was of course my grandmother but she was also like my best friend. She allowed me to talk to her about everything. If I ever needed anything I knew she was only a phone call away. She would scold me when I was wrong but she always told me how much she loved me in the end.

In 1999 my grandmother called me and told me that my dad was about to get out of jail and she wanted me to come and spend time with him. I refused. She begged me to come but she flipped the request around. She said "Well just come and see me'. Now she knew I would never refuse her. My mom and I drove over twelve hours to grant my grandmother's request.

I was cordial to my father when I saw him but I could tell nothing had changed. We stayed there for a few days. When we got ready to go, Grandma called me in the room and she told me she loved me and thanked me for coming. She then called my mother in the room and told her that if anything happen to her she had to promise she would look after my dad.

My first response was "What are you talking about you aren't going no where cause I need you". All she said was "You will be alright". We left and headed back home. The same day we got home my father called screaming in the phone telling me that my grandmother was dead.

Not even twenty-four hours. I could not believe this. I was so mad that I actually blame my father for her death. It seemed like she held on long enough for him to get out of jail and then she departed.

I know I was wrong for feeling the way that I did but it was how I felt. I even at one point remember entertaining the thought that he did something to her. I was young and I was angry. These were just my feelings. We packed up, rented a car, and headed back up north.

We stayed at grandma's house when we got there. I didn't even feel right being there without her. My father told us that he got up that morning and when he went to check on her she was already dead.

I just wanted to get through it all and get back home. I noticed that my mom was being a wife to my father. I couldn't even comprehend it. Then I remembered what my grandmother asked her to do. We left after the funeral. We were not back at home long, before my mom packed a bag, and said "Take me to the bus station; I am going back up north". She went back to him after all he put her through. I felt like it was just to honor my grandmother's last wishes.

GREAT GRANDMOTHER

My great-grandmother knew that if she ever needed me to do anything I was only a phone call away. I was lead to go check on her one day and when I arrived at her home she was barricaded inside. She was peeking out the window with fear in her eyes. I had no idea what was going on.

When she finally opens the door I immediately noticed that she had bruises on her. I asked her what happen and she told me that a young guy in the neighborhood had broken into her home, stole her money, and when she tried to pull her gun out on him he took it and hit her repeatedly.

I asked her why she didn't call anyone. She said she was told that she better not call anyone.

I picked up her phone to call the police and that's when I realized that her phone line had been cut. I had to go to a neighbor's house to call the police. The officer that came wasn't very polite and made it seem as if there was not much they would be able to do. I was furious! I failed to mention that my great-grandmother looked every bit of sixty but was over one hundred years old when this happen. She was never the same after this incident.

On another visit to check on her she had some burns and she said she was using the iron to warm her feet. After this time my aunt who was her representative decided to place her in a home. My mom and I went to go see her several times. My great grandmother had an incredible sense of humor, I thought.

She would tell my mom she was getting black and she needed to stop gaining weight. She use to tell me how she loved my long hair (it was a weave) and how pretty I was. My great grandmother was very important to me. After all when my mother left up north running from my father, my great grand-mother's home was made available to us to have a place of safety. From what I have been told, she fell in the nursing home and died due to the complications of that fall.

I went to my aunt's house and helped her as she planned her home going. I found out so much information that I never knew. I thought she was my grandmother but she was actually my step-great-grandmother. We also found her birth and marriage certificate.

We found out she was one hundred and four years old. I was angry at the nursing home for allowing this to happen and angry because my aunt didn't sue but I realized that the anger wasn't bringing her back. I called grandma my china doll for two reasons.

One because a man that was courting her bought her some china dolls and two because she looked like she never aged. I miss her so much but I know she is proud of me now.

My mother stayed up north for a while with my father and things went from good, to bad, to worst. My father ran through so much money it was ridiculous. Money does not make you better it enhances what ever state you already are in. My father was a drug addict and money enhanced his addiction. My mother was a drinker and from what I have been told by family, because of what she was dealing with, her drinking increased.

My dad owed people money for drugs and they were coming to the house at all times of the night while my mother was left there alone while my father was running the streets. Things got so bad up north that my parents had to move down south. I had no idea they were coming. I was riding around one night picking up some of my girlfriends as we were getting ready to go to the club. We saw a U-Haul riding in the area appearing to be lost and we laughed about it. I got a call on my cell phone asking me where I was, it was my father.

He then told me that they were down south at a gas station and that they needed to stay with me for a little while until they found a place. I went and met him and guided them to my duplex. The next day I contacted my landlord and she allowed them to stay in one of her apartment units across town.

My dad received several lump sum payments from my grandmother's death and the more money he received the meaner he became. My mom would always confide in me about the things that were going on but get mad when I would address it. I was trying to break up an incident when my father was attacking my mother. He had been out all night and came in high. When I jumped in between him he attacked me in front of my children. They were screaming. I actually had to go to counseling behind this because my mom was mad at me for protecting her.

I learned that no matter how bad somebody's marriage is they are like scissors and if you get in the middle of it you will definitely get cut. My relationship with my mom changed. She would still discuss some things with me and my answer was always the same "If you are not going to leave him, I don't want to hear about it"! They ended up loosing that apartment and moved to another part of town.

My dad started being very active in church and everyone in the church loved him. They even tried to help him get his life together and he was at one point. He had several positions in the ministry and played the part well. My father had people believing that he didn't drink or smoke and that my mother was a gambling alcoholic. He always had a way of flipping things around and making himself look innocent.

THE RAPE

I decided that I needed to get back in church after loosing two important women in my life, so I did. I was doing real well. I had stopped drinking, smoking, and having sex.

I went back to my roots of not wearing pants, make-up, or jewelry. Not saying that this was holiness but it was what I was taught. Six months had past; I was getting ready to go on a retreat with the church to Myrtle Beach.

That first night we had service it was awesome. Service was over and I was still feeling the anointing flowing through me. Everyone was talking after service and I walked over to the water cooler and this was the first time I heard God speak to me so clearly.

As I watched the person in front of me fill their cup with water God said to me "My words will flow from you like rivers of living water". He told me that he was sending me my Boaz and that he was about to take me through a process.

I was terrified because they didn't talk about God speaking to you and prophecy in our church. I ran through the hotel looking for my parents. I was told they were on the pier.

When I found them I was crying and shaking trying to tell them what God had spoke to me. I can remember them just smiling and trying to calm me down. When I arrived back home, the next couple of weeks were so exciting to me.

I had a promise from God but forgot that he told me I had to go through the process. I was sitting in my home one day and God showed me a vision of exactly how my husband would look, I told everybody I knew. Yet still I forgot about the process.

For to whom much is given much is required. Things began to get really hard for me, financially, especially since I left all my supporters alone. One weekend I sent my children to my mother's house because I didn't have anything to eat or drink in my home.

A day later I received a phone call from a guy I had met years ago in a club. He told me that a close friend of his got killed. He asked if he could come and talk to me.

We went out to eat and he seemed like a perfect gentleman. Afterward we went back to my house and we sat on the couch and talked. He asked if I had anything to drink and I told him no. He told me he was going to the store to get something to drink. So he left and was gone for about one hour. I actually thought he wasn't coming back. I definitely was not expecting what happened next.

I opened the door, he pushed me and he attacked me. He grabbed me and dragged me through the house. He beat me and raped me.

I fought back but the damage was done. When he left I ran to my neighbor's house and told her what happened. She called 911 and when the police came they ask me questions about the attack.

The police asked me what the attacker's name. I told him I didn't know his real name, I only knew his nickname. He asked me how in the world can I have known somebody for years and not know their birth name. He basically made me feel almost worst than the rape itself.

I explained to the officer that I met the guy in the club and we hung out several times but we were not in constant contact and that I hadn't spoken with him for a long time.

I was so angry with God because I felt like I was trying to help somebody and he allowed this to happen to me. I went to church days later and I told someone what happened to me. She told me that I had no business trying to minister to a man by myself.

She said" A man needs to minister to a man and a woman to a woman". She told me I left myself open to the attack. I didn't agree with what she told me. So I continued to be angry.

I went to a counseling center for rape victims that the police victims unit referred me to but, it didn't help. I was too angry but I know now that until you deal with your emotions you will never get to the root of the problems you are facing. At one point I asked the counselor if she had ever been raped and she told me no, so I told her in a very nasty way with some choice words that she couldn't help me. I left and never went back there.

That's all the devil needed was for me to turn my back on God but God never turned his back on me. The devil inched his way back in. I received a call from the guy that raped me.

He told me he was sorry and that he couldn't believe he did that. He said when he left my house that night to go to the store he went and did some cocaine. He said his life had been hell ever since he did that to me and that he had just got out of jail. I hung up.

I couldn't say any thing. I began to have severe panic attacks. If I thought I saw him I would freak out. I was scared to even stay at home so I was always over my parents' house. They had no idea what had happen to me.

I remember one night my dad asked me "Why do you have bruises on you and why you act like you don't have a home that you are paying rent on". That was the night I told him I got raped.

We did not tell my mom but my mother knew something was going on because my dad and I began to get close in a bad way. We used to drink and get high together.

Finally one day my mom was nagging me and I just screamed it out "I got raped". Immediately she broke down and she told me a story I would have never imagined. She told me how she was raped. She said she kept begging her rapist not to kill her because she had just had me and how she felt like I saved her life.

I started attending a group called total recovery at church. People were in that group for different things they needed to be delivered from. I was under the assumption that I was going as codependency which was to support my dad but I soon learned that I needed it almost as much as he did. I had already made up my mind that I couldn't forgive my rapist for hurting me.

I felt like I had given my life back to God but my rapist had taken that away from me. I felt nasty and unsaved. I had already been suffering from depression every since I was seventeen years old because of the abusive relationships, but after the rape, a spirit of suicide came upon me.

I had already tried to commit suicide two times in the past. The first time was because of the death of so many loved ones and my daughter's father putting me through hell. The second time it was because I was worrying about bills, my parents' problems, kids acting up and other relationship issues.

The third try was after the rape. I destroyed my house. I locked myself in my room, broke a mirror and took a piece of the broken glass and cut my wrist. I watched the blood pour out my arm.

I begin to hear snakes hissing. Then I heard God say "You shall live and not die, purpose not fulfilled". I was screaming telling God that he didn't care about me. If he did, he would have not let me go through everything I went through. He said again "You shall live and not die, purpose not fulfilled".

My roommate at the time broke into my room and when she saw what I had done she went and got my neighbor. They took me next door and called 911. I had been in the hospital several times so I really didn't care about going back. I had decided to just give up but then I finally realized that God would not let me die. God has spared your life as well because he has a purpose for you to fulfill. After admission to the hospital they filed disability for me for depression and all the health problems that I currently had.

I stayed in the hospital for three weeks. I felt like I was in jail. They told me when to get up and when to go to sleep. I was told until I participated in the program I would not be able to go home.

I was ready to go home so I participated in all the programs so I could be released. I decided then that I wasn't going to try to kill myself any more but I had a spirit of suicide that hadn't been dealt and because it was never dealt with, it invited the spirit of self mutilation to tag along.

I didn't know it, but when it manifested I had no control over it. I was so angry at God that I refused to even consider asking him for help. I notice that any time I would get stressed or be in pain I would cut myself. It was like a transferring of pain.

I tried to get myself together the first step was I got a job working at my kids' school. About four months after I got the job I started to feel sick. I was going back and forward to the doctor. The doctor never did any blood test. They just assumed that I was dealing with too much stress.

The doctor's assumed that all my symptoms were just in my mind. I missed so many days I got fired even though I had doctor's excuses. I just had gotten a new apartment when I lost my job, so losing my job just added fuel to the fire. It was so difficult for me to raise my girls in the condition I was in so my mother helped out as much as she could without my dad getting angry at her.

I noticed I was losing a lot of weight and I was always throwing up. It was driving me crazy because I didn't know what was wrong. I went to the doctor and they did every test I thought was imaginable but couldn't find anything wrong so once again they contributed my symptoms to stress. I checked myself back in the hospital because I thought I was about lose my mind and that I was about to die.

After two days of being there the doctor told me my thyroid levels were extremely high. During one of the visits from my mom the doctor told her that I could have died because it was putting so much stress on my heart. The doctor told us that I had mitral valve prolapse. I already knew about the heart condition but we didn't know anything about hyperthyroidism.

The doctor assured me that I wasn't crazy and that all the symptoms I had been experiencing was connected to the disease. As I got ready to get discharged they told my mom if I didn't take the medication that I could die because my condition was serious. The doctor referred me to a specialist. I took the medicine and I seemed to be doing better so I put off going to the doctor. I began to question family if they ever heard of the condition before because the doctor said that is was genetic but no one knew of any family members that suffered with it.

GOING TO JAIL

I started dating again. I dated a guy I knew from my past but I never really was interested in dating him, he wasn't very attractive. I start dating him because I knew that he always had a crush on me and he gave me what ever I wanted.

One day he came to pick me up to take me to my doctor appointment, on the way back home the police pulled us over. At that time I was driving the truck and the police walked to the window and said "Step out of the vehicle". As I got out he placed handcuffs on me and told me that the truck had been reported stolen by the owner. He proceeded to tell me that the tags on the truck were registered to another vehicle. I explained to the police that I was driving my boyfriend's car and he was in the front seat. The next thing I knew we were all being hauled off to jail.

They took us to the police headquarters first. After several phone calls and interviews the arresting officer came and told me that the truck was my boyfriend other girlfriend's truck and that her aunt saw me driving it, so they decided to report it stolen.

He continued and said that the radio in the truck was stolen and the tags did indeed come off another vehicle. Okay by this point I am ready to kill him!! I ask the officer was I going to be released he told me NO because I had an outstanding warrant for a fraudulent check.

I argued with him and explained that he was inaccurate but guess what, they locked me up and transported me to jail anyway. As soon as we arrived at the jail they had us all sitting on a bench for processing, I leaped up with handcuffs on and tried to attack my boyfriend in jail.

They grabbed me and processed me first and locked me in a cell by myself for the rest of the night. I was released on a PR bond the next morning. I made some phone calls to find out about the check. I found out it was a check written to a local grocery store for twenty-five dollars and that I had already taken care of it years ago. The check system company never resent for the warrant. So I spent a night in jail for nothing. I had to take papers showing that it had been resolved two and a half years earlier for the charges to be dropped but it still shows up on my sled report.

When I got out of jail I tracked my ex-boyfriend down and I did what Jasmine Sullivan years later became famous for singing "I bust the windows out his car". After all that drama my girl friend and I decided that we were going to find us some white man to date since all the black men seem to be all dogs or abusers.

I remembered that my ex-boyfriend, I got locked with, had bought me some weed from a white guy before, so I contacted him and we begin to hangout all the time and eventually started dating. I never had to pay for weed or anything else. I was riding around in a new Cadillac on 24 inch rims. He never physically or mentally abused me. I really did fall in love with him, not just because of what he did for me, but because of how good he treated me and my kids. I thought this was the right man for me.

I met his family and spent a lot of time at his parents' home. I was use to being in abusive relationships so I was the one who would try to start arguments. He wouldn't argue with me and that just made me angrier. I stopped trying to start fights once I saw he really cared for me. After a year of dating him I was going through his glove department box and found some letters from his wife. Yes, his wife.

I had no idea he was married. They were separated but, not divorced and he failed to mention it to me. He didn't think it was a big deal but I couldn't deal with it so I always brought it up. Eventually we had to go our separate way. I felt like that was another two and half years I wasted in a relationship but we separated on good terms.

When we separated I had to get a job because he paid all the bills. I decided I needed to go visit the doctor for my thyroids to make sure I could go to work. I was told that my condition was severe and that I also had an autoimmune disease called graves disease. I was told I had to have radiation treatment to destroy my thyroid gland and I would have to take hormone replacements for the rest of my life. I refused treatment until the graves disease had gotten so bad that the pressure behind my eyes caused my eyes to protrude out the eye socket.

I received the treatment but I was still feeling like crap. The treatment was a low dose of radiation. This treatment is called (RAI) Radioactive iodine. The doctor said it would take about three weeks for me to start to feel better. In the process I notice more and more of my hair was falling out so I started wearing wigs. At one point I had a total of twenty-three wigs. I had low self-esteem and I decided to take all my anger out on men.

THE STRIP CLUB

One day I was walking with my children home from school and I passed this strip club and I decided to go in. When I stepped inside I was surprised to see that the manager just so happened to be a guy I went to school with. We were close in school; we were like brother and sister. Our birthdays are the same day and year. I was a couple of hours older. I asked him about a job, he thought I was playing. He kept saying you are not going to work in a strip club. I told him I would and that I didn't have a choice. He told me to come in the next night to work. I called him the next night to make sure he was serious and he told me to come on in.

My play brother use to hang out with a lot of strippers and that's how I even came up with the thought of dancing. One of his friends came up with my name the first night I went in to work, Sweetness. I enjoyed working in the club, it was good money. I got so comfortable that I started going to other clubs to dance in and out of state.

Most of the girls in the club treated each other like family so I started hanging out with the other strippers. They explained to me how I could make more money by tricking so I started to sell my body. It came to a point where I would pay one of my girl friends $100 to go with me just so I would feel safe. The difference between me and the other girls was that they were hooked on drugs. The money they made went to the drug dealers.

I picked up on that so I started selling drugs to them. I was always making money. Even if I didn't make money dancing, I made it selling drugs. I didn't have to worry about money any more.

I decided to go and work in a new club that wasn't in such a good area but I heard the money and crowd was better. I didn't have a lot of problem with the girls that worked there either.

I only got in a physical fight with one girl. She was upset because I wouldn't let her play the poker machine. She was calling me names because of how big my eyes looked due to the graves disease and saying I was fat. I just ignored her.

The DJ called me to the stage and the song he played for me to dance off of was "Beat that chic with a bottle". After I got off the stage I went in the back to change and she was in there with some other girls and she started talking junk. Before I knew it I had snapped. I bent down and took my boot off and started hitting her in the head with it and when it fell out my hand I grabbed a bottle and broke it and repeatedly hit her with it. I felt bad after the fact because I could have killed that girl, I hurt her bad! We were both suspended but after that incident, I never had any problems with anyone else.

I met these two brothers that use to be bouncers at one of the strip clubs through the same stripper that gave me my name. I started to hang out with them even though I could not stand the younger brother. One day we were searching for some weed and they said they were going to call their cousin.

They said their cousin only sold good stuff. When their cousin walked in my house I almost lost it. I had told my friends and my mother years earlier about a vision of how my husband was going to look and this guy was the exact image.

At that time I wasn't looking for a man because of all the drama and trauma I had been through. I had the state of mind that I was going to use men the way I felt I had been used and abused in my past. I just didn't realize that I was still being used.

The two brothers had already told me that he didn't like strippers. He thought they were nasty and he had no respect for a woman who didn't respect themselves. His cousin also told me he didn't give any body any money. I took this as a challenge as I was very attracted to him . . .

I asked him to let me borrow some money and I would pay him pack. He hesitated but he did after I convinced him I would pay him back with interest. That was my excuse to see him again. I had to pay him back. I went to work that night. After I got off I called him and told him to come get his money. He came to pick his money up and we were inseparable.

I invited him to go to work with me after a couple of weeks of us seeing each other. He came to the club but he only stayed in there for a little while, he really hated the strip club.

After a while we officially started dating. All the girls at the club use to ask me how in the world I could bring my boyfriend to the club while I'm working. I told them it didn't bother me.

He never told me I had to stop doing what I was doing. He told me he didn't like it and he only came the few times he did come to make sure I was safe. I decided that I wasn't going to trick any more after meeting him. I couldn't see giving myself to another guy when I felt like God had sent me such a wonderful man. He was nice, smart, handsome, giving, a hard worker, got along with my children, and was close with his family. I began to be happy for once in my life. I was real happy.

MINISTERING IN THE STRIP CLUB

I remember one night I walked in the bathroom and a younger girl was in there crying. I asked her what was wrong. She told me she didn't want to live the way she was living anymore.

She said she was having some problems with some guys and owed them some money. I told her that she could stop if she wanted to and it might be hard at first but God said he would supply all her needs if she trusted him. She said she didn't understand how I would be making money when everyone else wasn't.

I told her no matter what I have done to make money I have always paid my tithes, offering, and sowed seeds. I told her it has been times when we get off of work I would leave, change clothes in the car and go to church. I didn't always stay but I dropped off my tithes. I have sat in church having a hangover from the night before but those were the messages that I remember most.

A couple of weeks or so had past from the time I had that conversation with her when I was in the club on a busy night. We had a birthday party at the club, it was so packed and the girls were running around like fleas on dogs. God began to speak to me right there in the strip club.

God told me "You can give out advice but can not take it". He said that I needed to take my own advice. I thought to myself "Man, I know I'm too high!" Then God said that he was going to supply my needs and that it was time for a turn around. I was thinking man I'm tripping. We are often good at giving advice but, we can't take our own advice.

I went and sat in the bathroom for a while to calm my nerves. I smoked another blunt and went back in the club and began to look around and really see how foolish we looked degrading ourselves for money that ran through our hands like water.

I decided to take my own advice that night. I decided I was going to stop dancing. When the club was closing that night I told everyone that I wasn't dancing any more. I said boldly "I quit".

No one believed me. I packed my things in my rolling suitcase and told them that they could have all my dancing clothes, and shoes. I left and I never looked back or went back.

My boyfriend came to pick me up and asked me where was my suitcase; that's when I told him I quit. He was so proud of me and I was proud of myself. Most of the girls that were dancers didn't have anything to show for it but, I did.

A month or two later I told him that I was about to stop smoking weed. The very next day I stopped smoking and after one week my boyfriend told me that he was going to stop too.

At that time we were still selling weed so we decided we had to stop selling and stop hanging around people that were still involved with it. We accomplished everything we said we were going to do.

Do not let people say that you have to go through a long drawn out process to be delivered. There is a process but I believe the length of your process depend on the level of your faith. We had faith and believed that God was going to take care of us. Jesus healed and delivered people in the Bible, some were immediately and some were healed as they went. I believe it's according to your faith.

A few months past and I went to the doctor. I found out my eyes protruded almost completely out the eye socket because I allowed my Graves disease to get so bad before going to get seen and receiving treatment.

I was told I had to have surgery to fix the damage that had been done. I had to have two separate surgeries to put my eyes back in the sockets called decompression surgery. It was a painful process. My boyfriend was my support and he never left my side.

We decided we would put God first in every thing in our lives. That's when God started to bless us. My boyfriend got a raise and a promotion on his job. Don't you know that when you leave everything up to God he will make a way out of no way? He will give you promotions that according to man you do not even deserve because you didn't go to school to get the education that others did. Favor had come upon both of our lives and everyday God was working something out on our behalf.

Marriage postpone

We decided that we needed to get married but, we couldn't get married until he got a divorce. His ex wife had stolen all his money and ran up credit cards and disappeared over six years ago.

He had filed divorce papers in the past but nobody knew where she was to complete the process. So being the woman that I am, I decided that she wasn't going to stop my happiness, I had to find her. I knew with today's technology that I could find her on the internet and that's exactly what I did. I found her on a people search for a small fee.

Once I got her number I had to figure out what I was going to say when I called her. After rehearsing a conversation over and over in my mind I decided it was time to place the call. The first thing I did was ask to speak to her by name, as I was a bill collector.

Once I verified that it was her, she asked with a nasty attitude "Who is this". I then explained who I was and asked her if she would be willing to sign the divorce papers. She wanted to know why he didn't call her. I simply told her because he was at work.

The thing that surprised me was that her only concern was if he was going to file charges on her. I assured her that he wasn't and the only thing we needed was the divorce papers signed. I then told her I would be sending the papers and she just needed to sign them and send them back.

A couple days after the conversation with her I received a letter from disability stating I had to go to court for my final appeal. I talked to several people about the disability hearing process and was told several times that it would be in my best interest to hire a lawyer.

I searched the phonebook for a lawyer and I found a name that stuck out to me so I called and set up an appointment with him. At that meeting I decided to hire him. He gave me a short five or six questionnaire form to be filled out by my doctor.

My doctor filled out the form and once I returned it back to the lawyer he told me I didn't have anything to worry about. He worked on my case while we waited for the hearing date. I received the letter that sent to my boyfriend's wife stamped unknown sender on it. She had moved. I was furious because we already had a wedding date set and now she was messing our schedule up. I had to go back to square one all over again. I searched for her on the internet with no luck.

So I called information and the operator was able to give me a current telephone number. I called her and she sounded more upset than I was. She wanted to know why he didn't call. I told her as I did during the first call that he was a supervisor and he was at work.

She told me to send the papers and to have him call her. I mailed the papers to her but, he refused to call her. We waited to get the papers back so we could file for the divorce.

PREGNANT IN MY TUBES

I went to court in December for my disability hearing. The Judge looked at all my hospital records and other paper work and said quickly that I was approved. My lawyer then told me I was getting three years of back pay. I also got full health insurance that was much needed. One month later at the beginning of January I took a home pregnancy test and it was positive. I scheduled a doctor visit and they confirmed that I was indeed pregnant.

I left happy but wondering how my boyfriend was going to take it. He didn't believe me at first but he was happy. On my second visit to the doctor he told me that something was wrong. My HCG levels weren't going up so they schedule me to have some test done.

In February the doctor told me that the baby wasn't developing and he thought that something was genetically wrong. He told me that the pregnancy would abort itself or I could have a DNC to end the pregnancy.

I didn't want to have the DNC because I felt like that was a fancy name for an abortion and I promised I would never end another pregnancy. I told the doctor that I would wait to see what would happen. My HGC numbers began to decline and I started to have a lot of pain. The doctor told me that I needed to have the DNC because I could get an infection and die, I agreed to have it.

They scheduled me to come in to have the DNC done in his office. On March 3,2006 I went in to have the procedure done and it was very painful. It was worst than the abortion I had years ago. I left the doctors office perturbed and very depressed.

The pain I was having before the DNC was still there a couple of weeks after the procedure. I went back to the doctor and he told me my pregnancy test was still positive and that my levels had not really dropped.

He did an ultrasound and nothing was there. He told me I needed to have surgery but couldn't tell me why I needed surgery. I refuse to allow him to perform a surgery on me with any explanation so I searched for another doctor to go to get a second opinion. The new doctor I went to did an ultrasound and some other test. He came in and told me I was pregnant in my tubes.

They rushed me from the doctor's office straight to the hospital for me to have surgery. I called my boyfriend and told him that he needed to get to the hospital and I would explain everything when he got there.

When my boyfriend arrived at the hospital the doctor explained everything to him. They had me on so much medicine that I don't remember much after that. I had surgery and the next day the doctor came in and told me that the pregnancy was in my tubes and it had ruptured. He even showed us the pictures of how bad it looked when he went in to do the surgery. He then explained that usually when this happen you lose your tubes but he said he was able to clean my tubes out and everything looked good. He told me because of my health conditions that I shouldn't try to get pregnant.

I went home. A couple days later my boyfriend's divorce papers came. We went and filed them at the court house. The clerk told us it could be a while before we got a court date. We prayed and continued to plan our wedding as if we knew it would all work out on time. God continued to bless us because we remained faithful to him.

I received my first lump sum payment from my disability in March. The first thing I did was pay my tithes, then we went to a car dealership and purchased our first new car together. We bought a Pontiac Grandprix fully loaded. We were so excited it wasn't just the first car we bought together but it was the first car either of us bought from a real car dealership.

At that time we were still staying in the house I was renting under section 8. We were discussing purchasing our first home when we got married because we knew that he made too much for us to stay on section 8.

PREGNANT WITH PRAISE

About two weeks before mother's day I began to feel sick. I took two pregnancy test and they were negative. One week later I went to church with my spiritual mother. On the way back home she didn't ask me, she told me that I was pregnant. I told her that I wasn't and that I had taken two tests that were negative. She told me to go to the doctor because I was pregnant. It was on a Sunday, Mother's Day when I decided to go to the hospital. The doctor ran some test and said everything was negative. I asked if he did a pregnancy test. He said yes and it was also negative.

I went to church with my spiritual mother on Wednesday to her Bible study. We talked on the way home from church. I told her how I had been feeling and what the doctor said.

She told me I was pregnant and to go back to the doctor. I went to the store the next day and got a pregnancy test. The lines on test were very light but it was positive so I called my doctor to make an appointment. I went in the next day and the test was positive.

By that time I had been on medicine for bipolar and depression for eight years. My doctor told me, by me being pregnant; I had to stop taking all that medicine. He said he was going to wean me off of it but when I left I knew I was never going to take it again.

When I stopped taking the medicine it was like someone had taken blinders off my eyes. I didn't have mood swings any more and I stop cutting myself. I would never tell anyone to stop taking their medicine but as for me, I just believed God!

I called my spiritual mother and told her as always she was right I was pregnant. She told me that I was pregnant in a prophetic season and it was a season of warfare and that the pregnancy would be hard and very discomforting.

I had no idea what she meant but I soon found out. We continued to plan our wedding. It was a week and a half before our wedding date when we got the letter saying we had a court date for my boyfriend's divorce. The court date was four days before our wedding date. It's amazing how

God is always on time. The day the judge granted the divorce is the same day we went and got our marriage license for our wedding.

I begin to spot at the beginning of the pregnancy so I was very scared. The doctors did an ultra sound and determined that the pregnancy was not in my tubes and that everything seemed ok but put me on light bed rest. I begin to have a lot of pain so I went back to the doctor. He asked me if I was getting some rest. I explained to him that I couldn't because I was planning my wedding and it was going to be in the mountains. The doctor told me that I needed to get some rest and he advised me that going to the mountains could actually put stress on my pregnancy because of the elevation. I heard him but I didn't listen. We had our wedding at a church retreat on top of the mountains. It was beautiful.

I begin to spot again the day of our wedding. My mom said it was probably stress related. As soon as we said I do, I went back to our cabin and laid down to get some rest.

When we got home everything that could go wrong begin to go wrong. There were some repairs that needed to be done to the house we were renting. Since we had gotten married we were no longer under section 8 and the landlord began to act real shady. He didn't want to fix anything.

APPRECIATE WHAT YOU ALREADY HAVE

My husband being the awesome man that he was, took money out his pocket, and started to do all the repairs that needed to be done. He told me he felt like God wanted us to take care of what we were renting before he could bless us with our own. In many instances we beg God to bless us with things like cars, houses, or a spouse but God is watching how we take care of what he has already given us. If you are faithful over the little things that God has given you he will bless you with much more, but remember that to whom much is given much will be required.

We decided that we were going to move because we were putting out to much money in rent and repairs. We talked and decided we didn't want to stay in an apartment and we didn't want to rent from any one else. We wanted to buy a home. We didn't have any idea what we needed to do to start the process of purchasing a home so I suggested that we attend a home buyer workshop. We learned so much information during the workshop and we met some great people as well.

I told my husband to ask his parents if we could stay with them while we searched for a home. They agreed to let us stay with them. The first place we applied for a loan was through a lady that we met at the workshop. She got us approved but the interest rate was so high. She told us that we didn't need to pay attention to the interest rate of the fact that it was adjustable, we just needed to get in the home while we could and that we could always go back and refinance.

This was so shocking to me because it went against everything that we had just been told at the workshop. I looked at my husband and told him that we should look around. She then told us we were trying to drink wine and could only afford Kool-Aid. I thought to myself "Wow, she has lost her mind!" Her statement certainly turned me off and I knew it was time to get out of there. We declined her offer with pride knowing who we were and what God said.

I knew our God could do exceeding and abundantly above all we could ever ask or think because we knew we had power within us. My husband's mother told me about a guy who was a preacher that helped his aunt get in her home. We met with him and he took us around looking at trailers. That was not what we wanted. Then he said we had to pay him $500 and it was non-refundable. I prayed about this person for two days and on the third day I felt a no in my spirit, so I let him know that we were going to go a different route. By this time I was getting a little frustrated. I was not used to staying with other people. I had been on my own since I had graduated from school.

My husband's mother gave me another suggestion, she told us to contact the company they got their house through. They approved us but, it would take them a long to clear the land and build the house. We wanted a quick fix and that wasn't the route for us to go either. I told them that we were interested and explained our circumstances to them but we had a time frame to find a home.

We went searching for a home in the area that his parents lived in and we saw a couple of places that intrigued us. I looked up the properties on the internet once we returned back to his parents' house.

In doing so I ran across different manufactured homes that were in the same area. I called the realtor and a Chinese lady answered. She explained to me that we would have to put a lot of money down to get into a manufactured home. We decided against that. She then asked me exactly what we were looking for so I gave her precise details. I told her that my husband wanted at least an acre of land. I told her that I wanted a fireplace, flat top surface stove, three bed rooms, and 2 bathrooms. She said she would keep her eyes open and be in contact with me soon.

The night before I had an appointment to go get an ultrasound my husband and I were talking about baby names. He had already made up in his mind that no matter what sex the baby was the baby name was going to be Praise. I asked him why and he said because he liked it and that it was one of his favorite rappers daughter name. I went to the doctor to get an ultrasound to make sure everything was going ok with the pregnancy. I had finally reached five months.

The tech that did my ultrasound said that she had never seen a baby that was moving around so much so early. She asked me if I wanted to know the sex of the baby, I told her yes.

She told me I was having a girl. As soon as I left out the office I called my husband at work and told him we were having a girl. He started laughing saying that he knew it was a girl.

That night he told me he was naming her Praise. I told Praise godmother that she was a girl and she said her middle name was going to be Unique. The baby had her full name at five months, Praise Unique. I really wanted a boy since I already had two girls but, I prayed that she would just be healthy. The loss of the other baby was still weighing heavy on my heart. I just wanted her to make it here alive and to be healthy.

SPENDING FAVOR

A couple of days after I found out I was having a girl I was sitting in my mother in law house and I felt a strong urge to call the Chinese realtor to see if she found a house yet. I couldn't understand everything she was saying so we made an arrangement to meet at a McDonald's. My husband and I went to meet her later that day and she explained to me everything that we would need to do before we can really start the process. Her first question was if we had a bank account.

She begins to ask me questions about our credit and I told her my score was in the low 500's and my husband didn't have a score. She asked us to meet her. I called my husband and told him we needed to meet her. He got off work early and we met her.

She had us fill out some papers for her to be our realtor. She then asked if we had bank accounts. I told her I did and I pulled out a copy of my bank statement. She told us that she knew someone who worked at that bank. She called him. It was 5:20 pm on a Friday and the bank closed at 6:00pm. She explained to the bank lender about us, he told her to bring us in.

When we got there they were about to close the bank. He pulled all our information and told us we were approved for $150,000 at 6.12% and that if we found a house he could have us at closing in two weeks. He then told me that my credit score was actually 425. He told us that people didn't know that if you have money in an account it is easy to get approved for a loan through that bank. He said people can get approved even if they put the money in their account to get approved and then take it out the next day.

Our realtor took us looking for a house the next day. We found a house. It was ok. It didn't have the security fence, fireplace, stove, or room we really had talked about. It was a three bedroom one and a half bathroom on 1.5 acre of land.

We went ahead and filled out the paper work to get ready for the closing. The day before our closing we found out that the seller had a second mortgage on the house. We had to start all over from scratch.

I drove around that same neighborhood and told my husband about another house I liked. We looked at it. I asked our realtor if she could let us see the house.

When we came in the house it had a lot of room, 3 bedrooms, 2 bathrooms, fireplace, flat top surface stove, deck, privacy fence, and 1 acre of land. It had everything that we wanted. We filled out the papers in the living room of the house; it was $130, 000.

It took exactly two weeks for our closing. The day of our closing I went to pick my husband up from work and the lawyer office called and said we only had to bring $171.00 to closing. Our realtor had the seller pay everything. If you have patience and let God order your footsteps everything will work out. That day we spent our favor and saved our money. I had money in the bank due to my disability back payment but we didn't have to spend a dime of it.

PREECLAMPSIA

Right before we moved in our house I found out that I had preeclampsia. I was gaining a lot of weight and my blood pressure would always be high. It seemed like every time I went to the doctor they made me lie down until my blood pressure would go down. The doctor said I should rest.

We moved in our new home and we were all so excited. I continued to get sick. The doctors told me I had to be on complete bed rest. I was five months when they started making me go to the hospital because of my blood pressure.

When I turned six months I got tired of all that bed rest. One Friday I had an appointment. I called and canceled it. The nurse told me I needed to come in for them to check my pressure I told her I was tired of driving back and forth to the doctor.

She put another nurse on the phone; she made me promise I would be there Monday morning. I told her I would come in. I went to the doctor that Monday. They made me stay there for almost two hours for my pressure to go down. It didn't so they took me straight to the hospital. I left later that night. I told the nurse I wasn't coming back to the hospital until it was time for me to have the baby.

Thursday I went to the doctor and I knew they were going to make me lay down. I told the nurse I wasn't going to the hospital. My blood pressure went up higher so I had to go to the hospital. The nurse took me to the hospital. The doctor came over later and told my husband and me that I would be there until I had the baby.

The doctor came in Saturday and said that if my test were worse when he came back Sunday he would have to do something. That night they gave me some medicine to make the baby lungs mature faster. My breast swole up and began to leak.

The nurse came in and she said she never seen this happen before a baby was born. She used something to bind my breast up and packed them with ice. Sunday, my husband, his mom, and the kids came to the hospital after church. They were about to leave when the doctor came in and said that my kidneys were shutting down and my blood pressure was so high they didn't want me to have a seizure so, he was about to take the baby.

My first thought was I just turn seven months today and I never had a C-section before and didn't want to have one. My husband asked when they were going to take the baby and the doctor said in a couple of minutes. I could see the fear in his face. I called my mom and dad to let them know.

While they prepped me I told the doctor that I wanted my tubes tied. They gave me the papers to sign. I talked my husband in to going in the operating room with me. The doctors assured him he wouldn't see anything unless he wanted to.

Everything seemed to be going good. Once they got the baby out the doctor allowed my husband to go out in the waiting room to let everybody know the baby and I were okay. The doctor was trying to get the after birth out but, it was stuck. I felt a lot of tugging. The doctor scrapped all he could out. They rolled me by my baby and she looked so little.

Physician heal thyself

I asked the nurse what did she weigh and she told me two pounds and six ounces. That night my mom stayed with me. I began to feel nausea. By the time I pushed the call button for the nurse I gagged but nothing came up. The second time blood and big clots of tissue came from my bottom. I begin to lose a lot of blood so the doctor orders a blood transfusion. I received three units of blood.

The next day I was able to go see my baby. She was on a ventilator and she had a feeding tube in her mouth. I was so upset when I saw her that I got sick. My blood pressure went up and stayed up. I had the chills so bad. I did not want to get out of the bed to use the rest room because I would be so cold. I was shaking. The nurse called my doctor to find out what they needed to do. He ordered some medicine through my IV.

I could tell something was wrong because three nurses came in my room. At all times there was at least one by my bed. She asked me who I wanted them to contact. I told her my husband. She had someone call. They said they couldn't get in touch with anyone. They had called the house phone, my husband and mother's cell phone.

I asked her what was wrong and she told me that my blood pressure was so high that I should have already had a stroke. I got my cell phone and I called my husband, the house, and my mom cell. No answer. I begin to get nervous. I was already shaking because I felt like I was freezing. I did not feel like I was about to die nor did I have the excruciating headaches I usually had when my blood pressure was high. I just felt extremely cold.

Two of the nurses left out the room and just one was left in there with me. I asked the nurse if she could get me the little bottle of oil that was in the dresser beside the bed and she did. I opened my oil and I anointed myself. I began to pray.

I told the Lord that I know he didn't bring me through all this for nothing. I told God I had to be here with my husband and my kids. I told God that my baby was sick and needed me. I begin to speak in tongues and the nurse was scared. I don't know if she thought I was going crazy or that I was dying.

She ran and got another nurse and they kept asking me was I alright. They had to call the doctor once again because my pressure had gone up higher. They then came back in and put some more medicine in my IV. After several minutes my pressure was still high so they administered more medication in my IV. All of a sudden I felt a sharp pain in my arm. As I grabbed my arm I noticed that it was ice cold and was turning blue.

I notified the nurse that was in the room with me and that's when they found out that my IV had infiltrated. The medicine was not going in to my blood stream. They had to start a new IV and gave me more medicine.

I continued to pray until I fell asleep. When I woke up, the nurse first made contact with my mother, who in turn told my husband what was going on. By that time I was feeling better.

Early that morning the doctor came in and I told him I wanted to go home. He told me that after that scare last night I needed to stay for observation. I made it very clear that I wanted to go home and that I was going home. My mother was in the room by that time. The doctor finally agreed that some people get more rest and heal faster at home but he said I had to be on bed rest.

After a while my mom and I went to see the baby in the intensive care unit. I cried because she was so tiny and looked so helpless. I must admit I was crying also because I didn't want to leave her in the hospital. My mother had to calm me down and encourage me. I breast-fed my other two girls because I knew the importance of breast milk during the first couple of months in a baby's life so I already knew that it was even more important for my premature baby.

It was stressful for me every time I pumped and stored my milk. I had to take it to the hospital to my baby that was on a feeding tube, praying that it would help her body fight even harder. The hospital was about thirty minutes away from our home.

A month after I delivered Praise, we had my baby shower since she came so early and we did not know if she was going to make it. My mom and I actually left people in my home during the baby shower because I wanted to go see Praise at the hospital.

Having the baby shower without the baby being home was a heavy burden on me. Even as I look back now, I can remember just going through the motions, being numb. I would cry all the time and my husband would always tell me "Baby it's going to be okay". He never broke down in front of me, he stayed strong for me.

The next day my husband and I went to go see Praise. My husband kept saying it look like she was breathing too fast. The nurse said it wasn't anything wrong. The following day the hospital called and said that Praise tested positive for RSV, her kidneys were failing, and that she also needed to have a blood transfusion. I was so upset because my husband knew something was not right but they refused to listen to him. I told him what the nurse said. He went outside. I found him on the deck and for the first time I saw him cry. At that point it felt like someone crushed my heart.

My mother and I went to the hospital the next day to find out exactly what was going on. I was told I had to sign some papers so that they could proceed with the baby's treatment.

Finally the doctor came in to talk to my mom and me. He took us in the family room. You know the room they take you in when they tell you your love one has died.

The doctor looked at us with disappointment in his eyes and told us that my baby was not going to live because her condition was serious, that she was extremely small, and it would be hard for her to fight through it. I cried, ran out the NICU in the hallway, and made some phone calls. I called my husband, dad, and my third call was to my spiritual mother.

My spiritual mother told me that it was not so. She said to me "What do we do when our back is against the wall". I muffled with tears in my eyes "Praise him". She said alright then I'm going into warfare.

It's not what it look like

Later that day, I talked my husband into going to the hospital with me to see our baby, as the doctor only gave her a day or two to live. When we arrived at the hospital we had to go through the ritual I had to go through everyday of scrubbing in. As we looked at her as she struggled to hang on to her life I reached in the incubator anointed her and we prayed. Her oxygen levels dropped and she stop breathing. They had to resuscitate her two times as we stood there helpless.

My husband had to sit down. We ended up having to leave, my husband couldn't take it. As we left, we walked across the cross walk and God began to speak to me.

God said "If I could raise Lazarus from the dead, I can heal your child who is still yet alive". I told my husband what God had spoken and we grabbed hands and we left believing God.

The hospital called and told us because Praise was having so much trouble they were changing her ventilator to a high power ventilator. They said it would loosen up the pneumonia in her lungs and breathe for her.

The doctor also gave her morphine so she would not be in pain. I knew that the situation was getting worse but I remembered a sermon that was preached that said it's not what it look like and some times it has to get worse before it gets better. If we never have a crisis in our lives we would never experience God's hand. Sickness, disease, hurt, pain, and even lack are things that God don't put on us but he allows so that we can say with assurance that He is a healer, deliverer, and a provider. He makes his self known in our weakness.

I went to go see Praise the next morning. I asked one of the other nurses what happened to the nurse that was caring for my daughter. I found out that the nurse that cared for her was sick and that's how my daughter possibly got sick.

She then told me the nurse had the flu and she had to stay off of work for a week but, my child was fighting for her life. I was tremendously upset, but God didn't even let me dwell on that.

The devil will do things to get us off focus so that we will not do what we are supposed to be doing. One of my favorite sayings is "The devil is doing his job, we have to do ours". So I got back to doing my job, praying without ceasing.

I continued to go to the hospital to anoint and pray for her daily. On two occasions I had nurses ask me what I was doing when I was anointing her. I had to explain to them what the oil represented.

Even as my child was laying there God was using her sickness to minister to others. The process she went through was speaking loud of God's mercy and sovereignty. It seemed at one point the harder we prayed the sicker she got but we continued to pray and had so many people in agreement with us in prayer.

The key is not just to murmur words that you really do not believe, but to believe that what you pray is already done in the spirit and to expect to see the manifestation in the natural.

I received a call from the doctor explaining to me that Praise had woke up even though she was heavily sedated and pulled the ventilator out and they had to put it back in but, she was ok. I told my husband about this and we looked at each other and said "She is a fighter". We prayed that night that God would give her strength to keep fighting and give her a speedy recovery.

I received another call, the nurse told me that Praise had pulled the ventilator out two more times during the night and the doctor decided to order some x-rays of her lungs and if they were clearing up he would try to leave her off.

The test came back and her lungs were clearing up so they left her off the ventilator but she had to stay on the oxygen and feeding tube. I said to myself "One thing down and two more things to go".

It seemed like as quick as her illness turned for the worst, that's how quick God turned it around and began to heal her. Praise began to gain weight everyday. Finally they let her try to drink from a bottle and she did well so they took the feeding tube out.

She had a lot of reflux and her oxygen levels would drop very low when she ate so she had to remain on a low amount of oxygen. They also put her on reflux medicine.

All the nurses would come and check on Praise because they couldn't believe she was the same baby that was fighting so hard for her life and how fast her condition turned around.

They had her spoiled rotten. Someone was always holding her when I went to visit her. About a week later they took the oxygen off and she was able to come home a couple days later on an apnea monitor. She was in the hospital for a total of three long months.

Two months after she came home I was having a lot of pain and my menstrual cycle would only stay off for four to five days before it would come back on. So I went to the doctor and he told me I need to have surgery.

I had a lot of scar tissue from the C-section and I also had four fibroid cysts. He told me that they would remove everything. I was having a surgery called Microdermablasion with Novasure. The surgery would stop my periods so I didn't have to worry about the cramping any more.

I got the surgery and it went great. I was able to get back to a normal life. Praise stayed on the monitor until she was seven months. At eight months I anointed her throat and stomach and I stopped giving her the reflux medicine and she is doing well.

In June my family went on a church retreat to Florida. It was during the same time of our first wedding anniversary and my birthday. God spoke to me and told me he was taking me to another level in him and I had to move out of my comfort zone.

God then told me I had to leave the church I was attending. I didn't want to leave because I had been there for eight years but, I had to be obedient to God. I told my husband that Gods wanted us to join his mother's church. He said "Okay". The very next Sunday we all joined the church.

There was so much love in this church. You didn't have to wonder if the love was real you felt it. Once we joined God began to increase in me.

I thought I was going to join and do what we did in the mega church. Well it did not work that way. When we joined, the Pastor asked us if we would pay out tithes faithfully and the next question was what our gift was to the body of Christ.

We have always been faithful tithe payers so that wasn't an issue but we never sat and thought about what we were called to do in the body of Christ. She was not in a hurry because she paused and waited for our responses.

This may sound crazy but my husband and I have a saying when we are playing cards "If you think too long, you think wrong". So the first thing that came to my mind was the training I received at the mega church we had just transitioned from. The women's ministry had intercessory prayer every Thursday and the president of the women's ministry, which was the pastor's wife taught me how to be a prayer intercessor and a prayer warrior.

Our new Pastor put us right to work. My husband was the Chairman of the Trustees and over the Media Ministry. I was over the Intercessory Prayer Team Ministry. The intercessory prayer and media ministry didn't even exist until we got there. So, we are a living witness that your gift will make room for you.

My daughters helped start the Step Team and Drill Team. My middle daughter also participated on the Praise Dance Team, and Choir. My husband and oldest daughter played the drums.

Sometimes it takes God to pull, push, or remove you from where you are just so you can stop hiding and find out who you really are in Christ. I later acknowledged the call into ministry to my Pastor.

She said that she already knew but she was waiting on me to come to her. She asked me what God was calling me to do and I explained to her that I had a dream and God told me that he has called me to be his Evangelist and tradition breaker.

I made this calling known to the church and began to take ministerial classes. After I started attending ministerial class I began to see my husband studying the Bible more and more. Then one day he came to me and told me that God was calling him to be a deacon and he showed me where he had been studying about a deacon in the Bible. He had one concern though. He read that a deacon had to be the husband of one wife and he was told that he did not qualify because he had been married before. I told him that he was the husband of one wife. I explained to him that the Bible says "What God has joined together let no man put asunder". I reminded him that he said he felt pressured into that marriage and the end result was his ex-wife running off with thousands of dollars and disappearing.

To settle the misunderstanding of the text and to assure him that he was hearing God calling him as a deacon, we went to the Pastor for revelation of the matter. She told him that he had one wife and also was able to give more detail scripture references so that we both had a clear understanding. After clarification and another week or two of prayer he announced his calling as a deacon and began training classes to be a deacon. The classes where scheduled to last two years.

I went to visit a church for a women's conference and my mother and one of my good friends went with me. It was there that I met the speaker for that night, a Prophetess who became my spiritual mother. During that service she was prophesying to a lady in the front of the church and the Holy Ghost fell on me and knocked me to the floor. While I was on the floor God showed me a vision. I saw a church decorated in purple and gold, with about thirty people standing inside. I also saw four people on the pulpit and my husband walked up and said "Everyone please remain standing while our Pastor come and greet us". I walked forward and said "Welcome to According To Your Faith Ministries".

I immediately open my eyes and began to cry saying "no, no, no". I was so upset because I was not trying to be nobody's Pastor. I knew I was not ready for an assignment like that. I sat there lingering between depression and confusion for a while when the Prophetess called me forward. She told me that I had been places and the prophets would prophecy to everyone but me, she said it was because I was a prophet. She told me that God had a greater call on my life but it would be manifested at its appointed time. I only told a few people about this experience because God spoke to me and told me "Don't tell my dreams to dream killers"! To me, I didn't consider that vision a dream; I considered it to be a nightmare. So unlike some people I did not go out and try to start a church based upon the vision I saw. I knew I was not ready and I was not going to try and make myself ready. I filed that vision on a shelf.

During the next few months while my husband and I were attending our leadership classes all hell broke loose in our life. There were attacks on my health, my husband job, our children and so much more but we remained faithful to the ministry. One thing that I learned was that we were being faithful to the local church, but was neglecting our own family. Every time the church was having service, we were there. Every time the Pastor had to go preach, we were there. Sunday school, Bible study, ministerial and deacon classes, we were there. I finally began to realize that my children had gotten to the point that they hated going to church because we were always there.

The day before we went before the board to be tested on what we had learned, I stopped by a friend's house to drop off some food on the way to church. As I was leaving, her neighbor who was a Muslim came in and asked her to pray with him. She looked at me and asked me to stay and pray with her, so I did. She began to pray and as soon as I said in the name of Jesus, the man began to growl at us. His skin color and even the tone of his voice changed. I looked toward the door to see if my husband heard what was going on because he was sitting in the car. He was not there. I reached my hand in my pocket and I pulled out a little vial of anointing oil. As I looked at the door again I saw my husband standing there so we proceeded to pray. It seemed as we were praying for an eternity and I was feeling like I had been in a ten round boxing match.

When we left we went to church and my husband went in the church and had the Pastor come out and she prayed strength back in to me.

The next day went before the board for our testing, we were both so nervous. When I went before the board they asked me the entire license questions and since I knew all the correct answers, one of the Bishops on the panel said to proceed to ask me the questions for ordinations including a mock wedding, funeral, and communion service. I went through those procedures and was asked to leave. We were not told who passed until official day. We both past and were ordained in the organization. The Pastor had us stand before everyone and answer all the questions again because there were some people that were upset because we had not been in class for the full two years and the board ordained us.

My husband and I was the first couple to be ordained under the organization at the same time. God began using me immediately operating in healing, prophecy, and to cast out spirits in Jesus name. I can remember praying one night and asking God why it felt like my cup was overflowing and he responded "It's time to pour out".

As my husband and I were obedient to all God commanded us to do we began to receive an abundance of blessings. I thank God for the spiritual increase in my family more than any of the material blessings we had received.

I am not telling you that everything went smoothly after we lined up with God's will because it didn't. The devil hit us with everything that he possibly could to attack us. I can say with assurance that because we were in God's wills he gave us enough strength to endure what was to come. Lord knows I had stored up plenty of prayers and praises in advance and I also believe that helped us endure.

The first major attack was that my husband was laid of his job that he had been working on for almost eleven years. He went to work one morning and after working half the day he was told he was laid off. I wasn't shocked because so many changes had taken place in the company.

I told my husband prior to this happen he better be careful of what he was saying because to me it seemed as though he had become a little prideful. One day during a conversation he said "I have a position that people have to go to school for years to attain, and I have never been to school to do what I do. I am the superintendent, they not going to let me go". Little did he know they were starting from the top in down sizing.

He had a lot of stress on his shoulders because he is the type of man that loves to work and take care of his family. I honestly think we made the devil mad because we refused to let him steal our joy even though we were going through this hardship. We praised God like nothing was even going on in our life. My husband did not do like some men and sit around doing nothing. He went and applied for unemployment and filled out applications for jobs the very next day. Since it seemed as though he would never find a job, he decided to create one. He started his own business, Healing Hands Lawn Service. He did everything from lawn care, pool and sprinkler system installation, and finishing concrete driveways. We did not have an over flow of finances in any sense but we were able to keep the lights on and food on our table.

I was receiving disability for myself and our youngest daughter, and he was receiving unemployment benefits. The only things these two incomes did were keep the basic utilities on. We didn't even have enough to pay for our mortgage. I even told my husband that I would get a job to help out but he told me he did not want me to work. He told me that it was up to me if I wanted to get a job but he preferred to care of the family. I decided to go back to school after having graduated high school fifteen years earlier. I enrolled in school for medical assistance.

My husband went on several interviews and every where he went he was told that he was over qualified for the positions. He even told them he would take a pay cut, they still said they could not hire him. One of my professors at school even helped me type up a professional resume for my husband and he also talked to some people that he knew in the construction field to see if anyone was hiring. He continued to go on interviews but he heard the same thing over and over again "Over qualified".

The second major attack was when my daughter was taken by the state for an allegation she made on my husband. My daughter was taken for words that were supposedly said. It was nothing physical at all. It was a case of he said she said. The case started because my daughter had already been locked up two times for incorrigibility and was on probation. She was basically out of control. She asked to go to a party and I told her no. I had to go preach at a women's conference out of town and she did not want to go, so she asked if she could stay at her dad's house. We dropped her of and when we went to pick her up that's when the allegations were brought to our attention. I told her that she could stay there until we figured things out. I called her dad and told him we were coming to get her and he refused to allow her to come home.

I contacted the police and I was told that since we had an upcoming hearing for her probation violation that we could address that issue then. I contacted a lawyer to find out what we should do and I was advised that it would look better if we filed the complaint to let Department of Social Services know that allegations were being made against my husband. My husband and I went in and filed the complaint as instructed.

As we prepared to go to court for the probation violation my daughter and her dad brought up the allegations of what was said, because I felt like her father was over exaggerating the issue because he was seeking custody. I told the courts about the severity of his past criminal record. All hell broke loose in the courtroom. I tried to stress the fact that my husband and I made DSS aware of these allegations and if her father was so concerned about her welfare, why he never filed a report of the allegations. The judge did not want to hear anything else; they took my daughter into the state's custody. I felt miserable and I had a sense of relief all at once. I was upset that they took my daughter but I was also relieved she was not with her father. I personally always felt like all of this was made up just so that she could stay with her father.

We had several meetings, hearings, and court dates. Even the case worker said on at least two occasions that my daughter's story was always changing and that the story her father was telling was totally different from the several versions that they had heard. It seemed as soon as the case worker was getting ready to try to help me get my daughter home, they took him off her case. She had several different case workers over the time she was there; she continually told them she wanted to come home.

Now when my daughter would get mad at me she would say that she did not want to come home but that was only because I refused to let her have her way. Her dad on the other hand let her do what she wanted to do.

One time her father and I were arguing because I told him that she went in her room and started breaking things that my husband and I purchased and he told me if she was in his house he would let her tear up the whole room if she wanted to because it was her stuff and afterward she would have calmed down.

I told him he was a fool and she was not going to be breaking nothing up in my house. I felt like I was going through a battle not just with DSS but also with my daughter's father as well. I can remember times when we were suppose to be discussing my daughter's welfare and we ended up attacking each other instead. It was not a good sight to see. I was so angry that I had stopped listening to God and I allowed my flesh to take over. Once I saw things were headed in a bad direction and my flesh wasn't going to win the battle I had to repent before God and apologize to DSS, my daughter's father, and the attorney.

The next time my daughter's father showed up to a court hearing, God spoke to me and said "Do not say anything let Judas hang himself". That's exactly what happened. He told them about every criminal charge he had and then tried to explain them away. So they pulled up his charges and determined that he was unfit. He tried to fight it and they played along with him for a while and then he stop showing up. He was more worried about getting locked up for child support than fighting to get our child out of the system.

He actually called me while we were waiting for him to show up for the hearing so he could prove he was stable enough to get her and told me he wasn't coming to court because they were going to try to lock him up for the large amount of child support that he owed. They had actually placed me on child support and I was not paying my child support either but it never stopped me from showing up to everything that I was required to show up to. They did eventually file charges on me for noncompliance because I refused to pay the state child support. They even threatened to lock me up. I was ordered to show up to court for not paying so I was able to get a public defender. The public defender told them that I was on disability and according to the law; I was not required to pay. They dropped the child support case and made it retroactive, so I owed nothing.

When we were finally able to go to court to address the issue of the allegations almost two years later, all charges were dropped. The case was unfounded but the state refused to allow my daughter to come home. We were told that she would be turning eighteen soon and she could sign herself out. Four months to them was soon.

Over those two years my daughter was placed in homes over two hours away from me and I had to drive over four hours round trip just to see her. Finally about three months before her birthday, they transferred her to my city and I still had to fight for us to be able to have three hour off campus visits during the weekend even after all charges were dropped. I was told repeatedly by lawyers if I had an attorney she would not have ever been in state custody six months.

In the process of all this I was still in school to be a medical assistant. The stress of everything that was going on had a horrific effect on my health to the point that I had to take a leave of absence from school. I was diagnosed with Interstitial Cystitis which is a condition that causes bladder/ pelvic pain and frequent urination. I was in so much pain all I could do was ball up in the bed in a fetal position and cry myself to sleep.

I also had to have my final eye surgery because of the Graves Disease. I had a real bad scare after my eye surgery because I was laying in the bed and I had a enormous amount of pressure in my eye and then all of a sudden I felt something pop and I couldn't see anything. I started screaming. My husband was outside at the time so I got out the bed and ran down the hall. I ran into one of my daughters and she asked what was wrong and when she looked at me she started crying. She beat me out the door and she told my husband I had blood coming out my eye. He brought me back in the house and gave me a cold wash cloth and we called my doctor.

The doctor told me that one of the blood vessels had ruptured and that I should put a cold wash cloth on it and if my vision wasn't clear in about thirty minutes to call him back. My vision slowly came back and by the next day it was clear again.

I had been out of school for a few months and I had no desire to go back. I was tired. I was tired of school, sickness, disease, and just all the struggles of life. I decided I had to force myself to complete what I had started. I wanted to prove to myself that I could come through the storm and test with proof that I did not give up. I wanted to show my kids that if I can go back to school and complete it, that they could complete the few years they had left in school. I also figured I would get a job after I graduate to help my husband with the bills even though he told me before we got married he didn't want me to have to work, but I am sure he didn't count on losing his job of eleven years.

71

My husband and I prayed about the issues that were going on in the church we were attending. We even addressed them as the Bible states but there were no corrections. We prayed and God released us to leave. We had a meeting with the pastor and explained to her the reasons we were leaving and we left on good terms.

We prayed for guidance and God lead us to help my brother in his ministry. My husband continued to apply for jobs and went on interviews. Exactly one month of us being at my brother's ministry my husband got a job with a smaller company but he had the same position making more money. God allowed us to stay in our home for over a year without paying a mortgage payment. Even though my husband received a job we were still playing catch up on all our bills so we still were unable to pay our mortgage on a regular basis. There were people that were four months behind that lost their homes but God truly covered us.

FILING BANKRUPTCY

We were told by a family member to file bankruptcy because it worked for them. We later found out that they had filed a different chapter than us because they didn't own any property. We called another family member and they referred us to a lawyer and went in for a consultation. We decided to file based upon the information that we were given. We had to make several payments to pay the initial fee before we found out what our monthly payments would be. Upon finding out what we had to pay we really felt like we were about to drown in debt. We were not aware that the trustee payment was going to be the around the same amount as our mortgage payment. We tried to make the payments but it was no way for us to keep up with them.

My husband makes good money but the problem was they did not always have work. He would go two and three weeks some times with no work between them finding construction jobs. No work means no income. People on the outside looking in just thought we weren't paying bills but they did not know my husband's job just did not have any work. We had learned how to go through our storms without everybody being in our business. We encouraged each other and ourselves. Why should you tell every body what you are going through when they can not help you, especially when their situation is just as bad?

We received a notice that our case was going to be dropped for non-payment so I contacted our lawyer and he advised us to switch our bankruptcy case to a different chapter. We had to pay more money to switch our cases over. We felt a little relief knowing we didn't have to pay that trustee payment any more but it made our mortgage to be over $20,000 past due. We received a foreclosure notice. I started operating in flesh again; I decided that we would try to do a short sale so we would not loose the house to foreclosure. I was concerned about how it would look to other people for us to loose our home in a foreclosure. We contacted a realtor and started the process for us to sale our home. We had several people who wanted to purchase our home but they wanted us to lower the price and I refused.

My husband and I decided that we were going to take our family, a young lady and her son who house had just burn down to the beach so that we could relax and clear our minds. As I was getting in the lazy river at the resort I slipped fractured my toes and had a contusion on my hip. I spent the majority of the time spent at the beach in the bed.

GOD GIVES SEED TO THE SOWER

I went to a service a few days after we returned home. A well world known prophet was preaching, he gave me a word of knowledge. He told me all about my health issues, past issues, financial struggles, all the way down to the amount I needed by the following Monday or my truck would have been repossessed. All I could do was sit there and cry. Later in the service he came back and told myself and the other people that came with me to sow $1000.

We did not have $1000 but I picked up my wallet and I had $41.00 and one other person had $2.00. People in the services were looking at us like they knew we did not have the money but we were still attentive to every word the prophet was saying. We can not allow money, the offering to cause us to miss everything that God has to say. He continued to preach as if he never even asked us to get $1000 but later in the service he stopped and asked how much money we came up with? We replied we are short $957.00.

People that were sitting, as close as two or three people down from us, began to laugh. If you notice we did not answer the question the way that it was asked to us. We let the prophet and everyone know what we needed. All of a sudden a lady that was sitting about four rows up on the opposite side of the church wrote us a check for the full $957.00. I praised God and I also cried because God had just made another scripture manifested in my life. He does give seed to the sower. The prophet blessed the offering gave us some oil and declared millionaire status over our lives. I left with my faith increased.

A few days later on a Wednesday my spiritual mother invited me to visit a church for a revival. The Apostle that was preaching during the revival had a level of faith that I had not experience before. He gave testimonies of the many healings that God had used him to perform and his teaching was with many revelations. During offering time, I went up to take my offering, moving slow because my toe was broken. The Apostle stops me and asked me what happen to my foot and I explained to him that my toe was broken. He asked me if I believe God could heal it and I replied yes. He asked me to sit on the front pew and he continued to take up the offering. After the offering he came over and kneeled down and said "Now let's take care of this toe". He laid his hand over my foot and began to pray. I felt heat enter in to my foot, and then I felt my toe snap, then pain went from my toe to my ankle, to my knee to my thigh and then it went away. The Apostle told me to get up and do something I was not able to do. I got up and walked back to my seat. That's when I realized I was not in pain. So I sat down and took the hard boot off, and I took the wrapping off my toes and that's when I noticed that all the color had come back into my toe and it was straight. The toe that was broken and crooked was actually straighter than the toe that was not broken. I jumped up and started praising God like I had lost my mind.

After service the Apostle told me he needed me to be in service for the remainder of the revival. I explained to him that financially I could not make it because I stayed thirty minutes away and I did not have gas money.

The Apostle who did not know me reached in his pocket and gave me gas money to be in service. The next day I called everybody telling them how God healed me. I went and picked up a couple of people and took them to the revival. The Apostle prophesied to me that night and told me that I was not going to lose my home. He told me to contact the bank about a modification. I told him that they had denied us for the modification but the Apostle said to apply again. He said that the bank was going to try and get us approved through the ne w modification program but it wouldn't go through but they would get us approved under another program. He then asks me to sow a $300 seed.

I looked around the church thinking to myself okay God who is going to write the check this time because I did not even have $10. Nobody gave me the money and I was instructed by the Apostle to sow it before the last night, which was Friday. I was thinking to myself theses people really do not understand how much debt that my family was in.

I decided to go on my Facebook page and go gleaning. I asked several people to sow a seed into my life so that I could bless the Apostle. I did not even collect $50.00 but I decided to just sow what I had. As I was getting ready for church I decided to check my bank account and that's when I noticed that the money from a gentlemen's taxes I had done was deposited into my account. I called and let him know that his money has arrived five days early and that I would drop it off after church. He then asked me how much I was going to charge him. I told him what ever he gives me is fine and then he said just take $300 out. I was dumbfounded.

I hung up the phone and started screaming. My daughter's god-mother was with me and I told her and she was just as excited as I was. When we got to church I could barely wait for the offering so that I could sow my seed. I know some people may be thinking "How could I be excited to give away the only money I had"? I figured if it wasn't enough money to meet the need, it had to be a seed. I sowed that $300 seed expecting a harvest immediately.

I did every thing that the Apostle instructed me to do but it seemed like things just was not working out.

A few months had gone by and we got the denial letter for the modification form our mortgage company. The Apostle that gave me the word about my mortgage issue was having a conference and I received an invitation to go but by this time it seemed like I would not be able to make it because my motor had went out in my SUV. I sent a text and told the Apostle I would not be able to make it. I received a call from his secretary telling me that they had made arrangement for me to attend the conference every night. His church was about one hour and twenty minutes away from my house. I knew God had to be up to something on my behalf to give me this type of favor.

VISION

The first night was awesome. As we were worshiping during praise and worship I saw a piece of paper appear with a pencil. The more I entered into worship the more the pencil sketched. As the sketched was being completed all of a sudden the sketched turned into the full picture of my dream house. I could not believe my eyes. As we entered into the service the Apostle preached the opening message and even though the word was awesome, I felt depressed in a way. I wanted to know why God would show me this house when we were struggling trying to pay for the home we were currently in.

After service I went in the back and spoke to the Apostle and he asked me what was wrong. I told him "I know what you told me but nothing is happening, they have given us a sell date". He looked and me, and I felt the whole atmosphere in the office shift. He said "Shut up, Are you not a prophet? How can you preach to the people about faith if you do not believe it for yourself? I know what God said so believe it"! I said yes sir. I felt like a child that had just gotten whipped by a parent. This was my fourth time ever being in this Apostle's presence but I felt like he tore my heart out and replaced it with the very heart of God. On the way home what he said to me replayed over and over in my mind.

The next day he had a well known Prophet preach. He prophesied to me and told me I was going to be a prophetess like none other. He told me that he wanted to bless me with ten of his videos and after I watch them to speak to my children, marriage, to my new place to live, to my ministry and to the jealousy of leaders. I felt everything on the inside of me shift. I did not know what was happening but I knew something was different.

The next day my husband and I went out to eat for lunch and every time our waitress would walk by I would see a vision of a little girl dancing around her. It started to kind of freak me out so I asked her did she have a daughter. She said she had one daughter and two sons. Then I asked her was the little girl four. She told me yes. God then used me to give her a word. She broke down crying. When she came back she confirmed everything that I said was true. She began to tell me the circumstances she was in. I ministered to her for a little while and then we left. I looked at my husband and said "I told you some thing was happening to me". Later that day I went in a grocery store and gave a worker a word of knowledge. All the way down to the name of the close friend that was in trouble. I can pause here and say I was terrified. I did not have any idea what was going on with me but also let me mention I was on a thirty-one day fast.

PROPHECY FULFILLED

A week later I received a call from the mortgage company stating we were denied for another modification but they got us approved under another program. They ended up canceling $25,495 that we owed. The representative told me that we had to come up with $1100 in two weeks for a payment and then pay our regular mortgage payment one week later. I told her that there was no way we would be able to come up with that amount. She told me that she would call me back in a day or two but she never called so I called her. I had to leave a message but when she called me back she told me that she had never seen it before but the manager agreed to waive the payment and they also gave us another thirty day to make our first mortgage payment. God worked it out just like the Apostle told me. My faith tripled but I also realized something, God worked it out when the words was spoken. I believe my faith had to be increased to see the manifestation.

My husband kept asking me when we were going to start the ministry that God had given me three years prior. I told him I was waiting on God. As soon as I said I was waiting on God, I heard God say he was waiting on me. We told my brother that we were leaving his ministry so that we could start According To Your Faith Ministries. Things did not go as smooth as I would have hoped them to go. I asked the pastor of the church we had been visiting to preach for our first church service and she accepted.

GO BACK

During a service we attended for her anniversary she prophesied to my husband and I. She told us that we were going to get a new car and it would be before our first service. I actually woke up one morning and God told me to go walking. I put on my shoes and walked about one mile when I finally heard God say "Today is the day, go back". I went and purchased a one year old car from the car dealership through my bank that had denied me three times within in last three months. I bought the car one week before our first service. The day that I graduated fell on my 4th wedding anniversary, and our ministry first service. So my pastoral and wedding anniversary is on the same date.

ATTACK ON THE KIDS

We began to see a lot of changes going on in our middle daughter. I did not know exactly what was going on but she was always angry and wanted to sleep all day when she got home from school. She went from doing well in school to failing almost every class. She began to use the phrase "I'm a PK and PKs are bad". My response to that was "The devil is a liar; you can be what ever you want to be and it has nothing to do with me, God gives you free choice". During this time my step-son was constantly getting in trouble in school as well, so my husband and I decided to allow him to stay with us. That happened to not be a good decision.

One night I went out of town to church, on the way home I got a call from my husband that our middle daughter and his son was missing. He called the police and they began searching for them. When I returned home from Virginia it was about 4:00 AM, my husband said they had just got home. I called the police to let them know they came home. The officer came and said they had to come in the house to make sure they were okay. I left him in and he walked around the house and talked to them to make sure all was well. He went and got in his police car and as soon as I saw him pull off. I went in my room and put my stuff up and I politely went in my daughter's room and told her to meet me in the living room. I got me a belt and tore her butt up. I did not care that she was fourteen and 5'11. I went for what I know. I heard God say look at her and when I looked in her face she was standing there looking confused and that's when I realized she was under the influence of something. I did not know exactly what but she looked drunk.

I was so mad at those kids and then immediately I got mad at myself. I was mad at myself because the words the Bishop had told me flashed in my mind. He said that family was ministry and everything else was assignments. I forgot to take care of family first. Everything was about ministry to me. I had to support everybody. I was traveling three to four days out of a week traveling supporting other people. Do not get me wrong when it came to cooking, cleaning, and all that other wife, mothering stuff, I did it but most of my time was spent in somebody's church.

I decided that day that I was going to take back the authority in my home. We have to understand that when we make a declaration before God, the devil also hears that same declaration and the devil is going to fight us tooth and nail to make us out of a liar. I decided that my family was coming first and who ever did not understand why I could not show up to every thing they invited me to would just have to get over it and themselves.

It seemed the more I sought after God the more hell broke loose in my home. I actually had people that I looked up to and valued every word that came out of their mouth tell me that it was my fault that my children were acting out because I was too strict on them. One lady told me that I was going to have to let my fourteen year old daughter just go and not to stop her because she would come back home. I realized something at that moment. I was receiving counsel from the ungodly. They had gifts but lived an ungodly lifestyle and secondly what works in your home may not work in mine. I understood the concept that she was trying to prove, that my daughter would have to eventually come home but, I was concerned about the condition she might be in when she returned.

Some people let their children do as they please and they turn up dead, pregnant, hooked on drugs and/or drinking alcohol. I decided to treat her as the prodigal son father treated him. I let her go! I refused to let her go and roam the street and do as she pleased in my home but I released her back into God's hands. She said she felt like she was in prison and did things intentionally to try to make me get upset. So I flipped the script and started laughing at the foolishness that she did. She would slam her door so I would take the door off the hinges. I would tell her she was on punishment and to not cut the TV or radio on, and before I could get down the hall I heard the TV cut on. I knew she was trying to provoke me to go off but I didn't. , I went in her room and took the TV out. Then I would hear the radio come on. I went to the breaker box and cut all the power off in her room. Okay, I must admit I wanted to knock her head off at this point but what put the icing on the cake was that she got a portable emergency radio and cut it on.

Then all of a sudden my stepson started acting like he lost his mind. My husband told him to stay in the room and to be quiet. He opens the door yelling. As I reached to close his room door back he snatched the door out my hand breaking one of my nails. I pushed him back in the room and he began to yell "Oh no, Dad she put her hands on me". My daughter really started acting up. She punched a hole in the wall and left out the front door. My husband packed up all his son things and took him back to his mother. Now I must pause here to say, instead of the mother being an adult she called me acting real ghetto. She told me I better not ever put my hands on her child but she put her child out for the very reason he was coming back home to her. He was very disrespectful. While my husband was gone I went into my daughter's room and found a shoe box full of liquor. I called the police and reported her as a runaway and informed the officer about the alcohol. The officer left to go find her. Before I threw everything out I took pictures of it. I also made copies of all the gang material I found in her room. The office found her and brought her back home and he questioned her about the alcohol. She told the office that she got it from a friend at school. The officer told me that he was going to follow up on the information.

The very next day I woke my daughter up and I took her to LRADAC which stands for Lexington/Richland Alcohol and Drug Abuse Commission. I signed her up to start taking classes. Things seem to only get worse.

On New Year's Eve we went to church and my daughter was instructed by the Apostle to sit on the front seat. She did so but you could see her whole demeanor change instantly. He told her that if he didn't come for no one else to be delivered, he came for her. He prayed for her without touching her and he called her by her real government name and she yelled out "That's not my name". That's when other people went to help pray for her and everything got out of control and by the time it was all over she stomped out of the church. We rode around and tried to find her but she was no where to be found. By this point I was on the edge of a nervous break down.

After we searched all around and could not find her I felt like I needed to go report her missing. I had some people telling me what happened in the church was wrong and that my child would never trust me again and that she would never want to go back to church. I was told by someone else that if I go to the police I was going to be destroying her life because they were tracking all the runaway and incorrigible cases that have already been filed on her and she was going to get locked up. I had so many people talking in my ear and I was so confused about what I should do.

My husband told me to go home and call the police and he would be there shortly because he had to drop one of our members off.

Well instead of going home, I ended up in front of the police office screaming and crying in the car by myself. I did not know what I needed to do. I could hear the devil saying "Just kill yourself, you're a bad mother". I found myself saying "But God said I shall live and not die". Then I heard the devil say "You care more about God than anything but he is allowing this to happen to you and your kid, go drive off the bridge". I said back to the devil "The fruit of my womb is blessed".

At that time my new best friend called me and I told her everything that happened and she asked me "Where are you"? I told her that I was at the police station. She said "I am on my way". She came and sat in the car with me until my husband could get to me. My husband and I went in the police station and they told us that we could go home and file the report. My best friend took one look at me and told me she was driving me home. Going way out of her way she drove me home. I realized that she was a friend indeed. She did not try to tell me what I should or should not have done. She did not place blame on no one but what she did tell me was that I needed to get in a quiet place and close my ear gates to people and only hear God. That is exactly what I did.

The next day was January first and I always do a thirty day fast in January. I was so stressed that it did not even faze me that I was not eating. We found out where my daughter was the next day and she did not want to come home. The police went to her location and made sure she was okay and I had to give the okay for her to stay there. So for the next couple of days I did not take any phone calls or even cut on my computer. I told the Lord that I wanted everything hidden to be revealed that was going on with my daughter. I went in her room and laid down in her bed and prayed and anointed the room. At that point I had a feeling that something was about to happen and it was not going to be good. I call her and I ordered her to come.

SHE STOLE MY CAR

A couple of days later my mother and a church member stayed the night at my house. We were playing cards and then all of a sudden a heavy sleep fell on me and I could not understand it. I did not say good night or anything, I just got up and got in the bed and went straight to sleep. Around 2:00 AM I heard someone saying to me "Wake up". I sat up in the bed and looked at my husband and he was asleep. I was feeling very panicking, like I was in fear of something.

I immediately began to bind the devil and pray for healing, covering, and protection. I realized then, that nothing was wrong with me, but something was not right. At exactly 2:15 AM, after praying, I woke my husband up and told him that some thing was not right.

Half asleep he asked "What's wrong"? At that moment all the power went out in the house and I heard the power transistor box outside making loud noises. I woke my husband up again and told him the power was out. He was not trying to wake up but he did mumble "It will come back on".

Then I heard some one walking in the hall, so I got up to see who it was. As I walked down the hall I saw my daughter sitting on the toilet in the bathroom with the door open. I asked her what she was doing with the door open. She responded "I don't know". My spirit was so uneasy. She would never go in the bathroom and leave the door open, not even to do her hair. I walked through the house and then went back in my room and as I sat down the door bell rung. I went to the door trying to figure out who was at my door at this time of morning. It was the police.

He said "Madam, who did you allow to drive your car tonight". I told him "No one, my car is in the driveway". He proceeded to tell me "Well you let somebody drive it because your car is around the corner wrapped around a pole, totaled". I pushed him out the way to open my door to look in my driveway and my car was gone. Immediately I screamed her name out. She came down the hall looking confused as if I had just awakened her up. I looked at her and I yelled "I know that you did not take my car". She said "What are you talking about I was sleep".

Everybody was trying to figure out why I was yelling at her, but they didn't know that I had just saw her in the bathroom fully dressed minutes earlier. She denied taking the car.

We had to get dressed to go around the corner to get all my belongings out of my six month old car because it was totaled! We noticed that there was a strong aroma of alcohol coming from the vehicle. My mother was constantly talking to my daughter trying to get her to confess when all I wanted to do was kill her. As we got back to the house I called a friend of mine that is also an officer. He explained to me that I needed to call the police back to come out and file a vehicle theft report because I did not know for sure who had my car and if it had been involved in any crimes. So I did as instructed I called the police to file the report. While I was in the living room with the police filing the report, my mother came to me and said call an ambulance, because your daughter admitted that she was drinking and that she did wreck the car and she is in pain. The officer radioed for an ambulance. While waiting for the ambulance to arrive I asked the officer could he do a breathalyzer test on my daughter since we knew that she was the one who stole my car and if he was going to lock her up. He told me NO and No.

Even after her admitting to the officer that she was drinking, that she did steal my car and wreck my car, I was told because she was fourteen they could not arrest her. I told the officer they are basically telling the youth that they can get a way with almost everything but murder. If that had been an adult they would have been in handcuffs as soon as they would have admitted it. He gave me that scripted response "I understand your frustration and we are aware some laws do need to be changed". All that did was irritate me even more.

Once the ambulance arrived they checked her out and said that we should take her to the hospital. They told me it would be cheaper if I took her. They said it appeared to them that her collar bone was shattered. She had several cuts and bruises, and she had a knot in the top of her head. Being that my car was totaled I had to wake my neighbor up to take us to the hospital. I know what I am about to say is going to shock most people but I knew she was alright and I wanted to have her butt locked up. Even after she stole my car, totaled it, and almost killed herself she still had a jacked up attitude as if we did something to her. I'm trying to ask her questions about what happened and she was raising her voice yelling at me.

When we arrived at the hospital I registered her and had to explain to them why we were there. My daughter had an attitude saying I'm always telling her business. Since I was already heated, I looked at her and said "You do not have any business, you just totaled my car". They got us to the back quickly. While waiting on the doctor, I tried to find out once again what happened. The only answers she would give me were I do not know and I do not remember. After her response my mother gave me the answer to the questions.

I asked my daughter "It's mighty funny that you don't remember anything but you have told my mother all the details". She yelled at me and told me she did not want to talk about it. I told her since she rather talk to my mom then I was leaving. I got my things and left her at the hospital. I called my best friend and told her what happened and she told me to stop walking and that she was on her way to get me.

By the time she got there the Holy Ghost had begun to whip my tail. The Holy Ghost reminded me of all the trouble I got into when I was younger and how my mother never turned her back on me. So I had my best friend to take me back to the hospital to get them. The doctor said that she had several lacerations, a mild concussion, and she only had a bruised collar bone. He gave her some pain medicine and explained to me that it can take six to eight weeks for her collar bone to heal.

I was still trying to justify my actions based on my daughter's actions. I told the Holy Ghost that I had every right to feel the way I felt and I never took my mother through half of the things my daughters' had taken me through. I began to remind the Holy Ghost that I was dealing with a child that got kicked out of school for drinking in middle school, was constantly getting suspended out of school, that was disrespectful, that had punched holes in my walls, and now had totaled my new car.

Let me make it clear, she was punished. I never spared the rod on my children. I even sought help from counselors, organizations to help youth stay out of gangs, drug and alcohol abuse agencies, and I even enrolled her in a program to have her locked up over night two times as a scare straight method but none of that worked with her. I went to the police station and spoke with officers there on several occasions seeking help but I was given the run around for the most part. There was one officer that checked on her and even did a couple school visit.

While we were home that day my mother, my church member and I was sitting at the table discussing what happened. All of a sudden I started laughing uncontrollably and then my member started laughing. My mom looked at us and said "What are you laughing at nothing is funny". I looked at her and told her "The joy of the Lord is my strength, laughter does good like a medicine, and I laugh in the devil's face because he tried to kill my daughter this morning, but God blocked it"! I jumped up and gave God praise. At that point I felt something shift in me. My faith elevated to another level after that confession out of my mouth.

Everything hidden revealed

Over the next couple of days I did a lot of running around. Believe it or not my daughter still had a jacked up attitude. I went to see if we could get her in an inpatient program for the alcohol abuse. My daughter finally admitted that she needed help and agreed to go in the program. They summited the paper work and told me that I should hear something within a couple of days. I went through the house praying that night. I told God that I wanted my daughter to be delivered and that I wanted to get to the root of the problem, so I commanded that everything that was hidden be revealed.

The next day I had a lot of things to do as my husband was leaving to start working out of town. That afternoon when my daughter and I arrived back home, my neighbor that had drove us to the hospital, walked over and started talking to me. My daughter went in to the house. My neighbor asked me how she was doing and what caused her to plummet down this path because she always knew her to be so respectful. I began to explain to her that I had been having some problems with her. I went as far as to pulling out my cell phone and I showed her all the pictures I took of where she had punched holes in three of my walls and how I had found all that alcohol in her room under her bed.

While I was talking to the neighbor my husband was packing up to leave to go work out of town. I was frustrated that he had to leave plus I was home without a car. That is when all hell broke loose. My neighbor said" Oh my God, I hate to tell you this but last month our new neighbor house was broken into and that alcohol looks like what was stolen out of her house". She explained to me that the lady was from overseas and the alcohol was brought from overseas and it was not even sold here in the states. I told her to call the neighbor and ask her what all was stolen from out of her home.

She came back with a list of things that was stolen. As soon as I saw the list there were several items on there that I know I had seen in my daughter's room. I had even asked her where it came from and she said that

90

a friend at school gave them to her. That story didn't sit well with me when she told me that but I could not prove otherwise so I left it alone. By this time the neighbor whose house was broken into pulled up and we called the police. Yes I said we called the police because by this point I was fed up and I realized what I had prayed the day before had just been manifested.

That's why people say be careful of what you pray for because you might just get it.

The police went in to my daughter's room and woke her up. They asked her what was going on and she said she did not know. She thought they were there to arrest her for the car wreck. That's when they asked her about the house break in. My daughter came up with the craziest story. She told them the night we left her home she saw a man running from over there so she went over there to check it out and she saw that the door was open so she went in and looked around and then left. They asked her did she take anything she said no.

I reminded her about the alcohol I found under her bed that she said she got from a boy at school. I informed her that we know that she took the alcohol from the house because it was imported from overseas and that they did not even sell it here. One of the officers took her outside to talk to her and my daughter finally broke down and told her that she did indeed break in our neighbor's house.

The officer brought my daughter back in the house and she began to go through her room and she gave the officer most of the things that she stole. The officer then told her that they were going to take her to the station to get her statement. For the first time, as I looked at my daughter being taken away to jail, it actually looked like she had peace. Until we confess the wrong we have done and if the wrong was done to hurt someone, we apologize to them, we will be vexed but as soon as you make things right by repenting to God and that person the peace of God overshadows you. Yes, I felt bad that my daughter was being arrested but I knew that this would be a wake up call for her.

I called the officer that I knew and he told me that they could possibly charge her with a felony because of what time she broke into the house it was after 11:00 PM and because of the value of the things that were stolen.

WRITING TO THE ANGEL

I had a day to prepare before she went before the judge. I continued to fast and pray and during my prayer, God instructed me to write a letter to the angel in the court room. I sat down and I began to write to the angel in the court room. I asked the angel in the court room to set the atmosphere for God to work a miracle out on my daughter's behalf. I then made my request known unto God. I asked God to allow my daughter to be sentenced no more than forty-five days and to allow them to provide the counseling that she needed to get over her issues. I asked God to turn the heart of the king, which in this case, was the judge. When we went to court the judge addressed all of my daughter's charges which were second degree burglary, petty larceny, possession of a stolen vehicle, and incorrigibility. Since she pleaded guilty she received a lesser charges and was only sentenced for forty-five days. Exactly what I asked for is what my daughter received.

My daughter was going to have to spend her fifteenth birthday in a juvenile facility. As one daughter was being locked up another was signing herself out of a group home to come home. I told God that I wanted all my children home, not one coming and one going. My girls have always seemed as they would take turns being on punishment. Every year, we would go to Myrtle Beach, my middle daughter would be in trouble and would not be able to go and when we would go to Florida my oldest daughter would not be able to go.

My daughter adapted well, being back at home. I did not have any major problems with her. The only issue we had was that she was supposed to be on medication for bipolar but she refused to take it when she came home. So I had to deal with extreme mood swings. She also had a habit of sleeping all day and staying awake all night. We had a conversation about her future. We were trying to find out if she was going to go back to high school or if she was going to get her GED. While she was in the group home she was constantly having conflicts at every school they enrolled her in to the point that she moved around a lot. Sine she was always being moved to new homes and schools she was not receiving her credits in school. So now that she was home she only had enough credits to be placed in the tenth grade. She decided that she did not want to spend two more years in high school. She decided to go to adult education to get her GED.

I did not go to visit my middle daughter one day while she was in the juvenile facility because it was located over one hour a way and my insurance company was still working on replacing my car that was totaled. She did real well while there, which allowed her to be able to call home every week. She even wrote me a letter of apology. I was just relieved that she was getting her system clean from the alcohol and drugs so that she would be able to think clear.

GETTING A NEW VEHICLE

I was able to eventually get a rental car so I decided to start looking for a new vehicle. My bank was running a special so I wanted to be in a car within two weeks before the special ended. I submitted two vehicles to the bank and they would not approve them because it was more than the amount I was approved for. I was so frustrated because I knew what I wanted and I knew that God said that I could have what ever I said. I went online and I found an SUV that I really liked. It had the third row seating. I called the dealership on that Friday and asked them to submit it to my bank.

The manager from the bank called me and was extremely rude. He told me that they would not approve anything over $15,000 and if I submitted $15,001 it would get denied. I asked the manager if I could pay the difference and he yelled "No, so stop wasting my time submitting vehicles over the amount approved". I felt like a little child getting yelled at by their parents when I got off the phone with him. I called my husband very upset by how the manager of the bank had spoken to me.

My husband being the great man he is simply said to me "Don't worry about it, it's not what he says it is what God tells you that matters, and if God said you can have the car you want then it's yours". I have a saying that I say when things really frustrate me, and I expect God to work it out on my behalf when I say it. I hate to say it some times because I have had people hurt me to the core and when I make the statement God deals with them. It's nothing deep but I found it to work. So I decided to say my saying to get God's attention to work this issue out. I looked to the heavens and I said "God this one, is on you, thanks for handling it"!

I went to my Apostle's church on Sunday and he gave me a prophetic word that everything was going to work out on my behalf. I am a praiser so I praised God like it was already done. You have to understand that if God sends one of his servants to give you a word your response can determine if and when you will see the manifestation of it. Prophecy is conditional. Early Monday morning I received a call from the manager at the bank and the first thing he said to me was "I apologize for the way that I spoke to you on Friday". He then proceeded to tell me "I don't know why but God had me pray for you this weekend that everything would work out for you, I resubmitted the SUV you sent in and I am waiting on management to get back in contact with me and I will give you a call later".

He called me back about four hours later and told me that they have everything approved and the dealer would be calling me shortly. The only problem was that my car insurance had not paid the vehicle off that was totaled and that had to be done first. I called the insurance company and I had to fax them the police reports and additional papers. The insurance company called the bank and told them that the check was in the mail. Then the car dealership called and told me that I could not take possession of the truck because my husband had to sign the paperwork and we needed to pay the down payment. She also told me that there was someone there filling out paper work on the truck I wanted and stated they would bring the deposit back in the morning.

My husband was working out of town, and was not scheduled to come back until Thursday or Friday. I looked up and told God once again "This one is on you, thanks for handling it". I received a call from the car dealership stating that they had spoken with the bank and the bank told them to go ahead and release the truck to me. She told me to hurry up and come pick my new truck up. I rode off the lot without paying the down payment or without my husband signing any papers. I believed since I could not put it in my name because of my credit, and because my husband was out of town, that God put it in his name. Once my husband got home we went to the bank to sign the papers and were prepared to pay the down payment. The manager then informed us that because we had gap-insurance, they were able to use some of the extra money that was left over from paying the totaled car off on our down payment, so we did not have to put much down.

Exactly one week later I went to see Prophet Carn and purchased his prayer cd. God instructed me to play the cd for seven days on repeat believing that God was going to release my daughter early. On the eighth day I received a letter stating that my daughter was being released early for good behavior.

On the day she was released the judge ordered one year of probation, $500 restitution, alcohol and drug counseling, individual counseling, gang prevention counseling, STD/HIV classes, she was required to keep her room clean and cook one meal a week. As soon as she was released and we got in the car, she told me that she wanted to go to church.

I was exhausted and really did not feel like going so I told her that we would go tomorrow. Everyone was calling to check on her once they found out she was home and she made it a point to mention to everyone that she wanted to go to church but I would not take her. My husband even told me "You know you wrong, if she wants to go to church, I think you should take her". So I told her to get ready. She was so excited! She kept yelling "For real, for real, we're going". I was so confused because this was the same child that was always complaining about going to church and now she was begging to go.

We went to a revival that was being held at my Apostle's church. They had an out of town speaker. During service he called my daughter out and gave her a prophetic word and asked her if she wanted to be delivered. She said "Yes", and broke down crying. That night was the beginning of the rest of her life. He prayed with her and she was delivered. Even her skin tone lightened up immediately, she had a glow. Even though the preacher was from out of state and staying in a hotel, he told one of his members that traveled here with him to do my daughter's hair the next day. He told my daughter that she was beautiful and he wanted her to come back dressed up with her new hair and told her that God was going to complete the work he had started that night. He said that God was not just giving her a outside maker over but he was also making over everything about her.

I realized that there are times when we really do not want to push pass over tiredness, sickness, depression, or frustrations to go to church, but we could actually be getting ready to cause our future to be null and void. I could have stayed home because I was tired. I had been at the court house from 9:00 Am until 4:30PM, and I really just wanted to rest and spend time with all my children under the same roof. If I would have stayed home I would have caused my daughter to miss her day of deliverance. She rededicated her life to God that day.

I thought all was going to be well since I finally had my family back together but I began to have some trouble with my oldest daughter. She felt like she did not have to tell people where she was going because she was eighteen. I also noticed that she would always jump in when I was trying to correct my other children. Things were beginning to get out of hand and I explained to her that she would not run my house. I told both of my older girls that while they were gone my house had peace and while they were here I would have peace and if they could not keep peace they would have to go. My daughter ended up moving in with a family member. Since she has moved out it has actually made our relationship better.

God healed me again

I am going to share one more testimony before I wrap this book up. My mother had a roommate that passed way from cancer. So it was extremely hard for her to keep up with her bills. She got evicted and my husband and I went to help her move. While moving some very heavy things I began to feel ill. I started having chills. When we got home I told my husband that I was not feeling well and I went straight to bed. My husband was leaving at 4:30AM the next morning to go to work out of town. I woke up in the middle of the night and was having pain in my bottom. I decided to go to the hospital.

When I arrived I was the only person in the waiting room. I went in the back to have my vital taking and my blood pressure was elevated, it was 181/113. I was placed in the room and told to undress. The doctor came in and did an exam and he told me that I was going to have to have surgery. I asked why and when? The doctor told me that I had a blood clot. I was confused. He then asked me if I had been lifting heavy object and I told him yes. He said that's what has caused this. I had to call my husband to let him know #1 that I was at the hospital #2 my blood pressure was up, #3 and that I had to have surgery. I could hear the panic in his voice. By the time my husband and his mother arrived they had already removed the plum size clot.

A week later after surgery I did not have a bowel movement. I had taken several things and nothing worked. I had to go the hospital because I was impacted and they had to remove the feces. After this procedure I began to have extreme buttocks and anal spams. I went to go see the doctor and he scheduled me to go back in the hospital to have surgery. The doctor was looking for a fissure. After surgery I was told that I had to have a solution injected and that should fix the problem. Now it had been two weeks since surgery and again I had no bowel movement. I had used everything over the counter that the doctor told me to. I took a fleet and nothing came out so my mother in law took me to the hospital. I felt like I was dying.

The doctor wanted to do a test on me but they could not get a line started. I was stuck a total of twelve times by two nurses, the doctor, and anesthetist and they still were unable to get a vein. The anesthetist told me that they were going to have to stick it in my neck. I told them "No you are not". I explained to them, that when I had to have my emergency hysterectomy I went through the same problem and they placed it in my neck. When it was time for me to be discharge, they pulled it out, and my body went into chills. I told them something wasn't right but they discharged me anyway. By the time my husband got me home I had a temperature of 104, so he had to take me back to the hospital. I was told that I had an infection and ended up in the hospital another seven days.

So I wanted them to know that I was not going back through that again. They told me that it was not much they could do if I was refusing treatment. They decided to give me a fleet and some pain medicine. After twenty minutes I still had not released anything. They gave me another one and a small amount came out. I told them I wanted to be released. I called my doctor later that day and made an appointment to see him. When I finally went in to see the doctor he told me that I had polyps removed during my last colonoscopy and he felt like a lot of the issues I was having was due to scar tissue from all the previous surgeries I had to have. He told me that he wanted to do another surgery to cut out the portion of my bowel that was damaged and depending on how much damage was done I may have to have my colon removed.

At this point I had gone through two surgeries in one month and now the doctor is talking about another one. I had been out of church for thirty days on complete bed rest. I called my Apostle and told him that some kind of way I was coming to church, and I wanted him and his wife to pray with me and I explained to him what the doctor said. I called my husband next and told him what the doctor said but I then told my husband that God was going to heal me and that I refused to have another surgery. I told my husband he had to get me to church Sunday.

I went to church Sunday, my Apostle and his wife prayed for me. He also instructed me to come back for communion because God was going to heal me. I went back and God had Apostle to serve me a double portion of communion and also he poured oil in the ram's horn and anointed my head. I felt the fire of God hit me so strong and I knew then I was healed. Over the next week I was still having symptoms but I kept telling myself "It's not what it look or feel like". Then one night God woke me up at 2:00 AM and said "Physician heal thyself". I got up and went in the front room. This was the first time I was walking unassisted since my two surgeries. I began to pray. I laid hands on myself and began to call out all the sickness.

I heard God say "Remember what your Apostle's wife said". I thought about it and she said "Praise will work in any given situation". God then said "Praise me now"! I worked myself out the chair and I began to move my feet while holding on to the chair. Before it was all said and done I was shouting all over my living room, healed in Jesus name!!!

There are many people who are church goers but, don't have a relationship with God. They know of him but, don't know him. They have been around his presence but he does not dwell in them. To have an intimate relationship with God you have to first be saved.

To be saved is so simple, in Romans 10:9 it states "If thou shalt confess with thy mouth the Lord Jesus, and shalt believe in thine heart that God hath raised him from the dead, thou shalt be saved". If you really believe what you confess you will repent. To repent means to change your ways, to feel sorrow, regret, or contrition for, or to change one's mind. Allow yourself to go through a sanctification process.

Contrary to popular belief sanctification has nothing to do with what you wear. Sanctify mean to make holy, to free somebody from sin, and to officially approve something. The Bible says in "1 Thessalonians 5:22 Abstain from all appearance of evil. And the very God of peace will sanctify you wholly (totally)". Also in Romans 12:1 it states "I beseech you therefore, brethren, by the mercies of God, that ye present your bodies a living sacrifice, holy, acceptable unto God, which is your reasonable service." Sanctification is where you put in work!!

Then you have to receive the gift of the Holy Spirit. To receive His spirit you just have to accept the gift that has already been paid for in full. It is a gift, receive it. You have to study God's word. When you are dating someone you spend time with them, to try to get to know them right? You have to do the same with God. You have to spend time with him to get to really know him and his will by praying, praising, worshipping, and studying his word.

Everything that God promised you it will come to pass, it's not according to our timing; it's according to God's timing. All things are also done according to our faith. I pray that my testimony helps somebody get through whatever they are going through or what they will have to go through. I pray that it help increase your faith so that you can stand firm and say "God is not a God of respecter of persons, if he did it for her, I know he can do it for me".

I didn't write this to glorify the devil but to glorify God. I want you to know that the battle isn't ours it is God's and He will always win, so why are you worrying. He said that he is a burden bearer so all we have to do is give all our problems to him. God said that he will forgive us of our sins but we have to first ask for forgiveness. A lot of times we know we are doing wrong but we never go to God and ask him to forgive us. We also sometimes ask for forgiveness but don't intend on stopping whatever we are doing. You have to change. You have to make an effort to do things different. We wonder why things haven't changed because we are doing the same thing.

You can't do the same thing and think you will get a different result. You have to do things different. We have to also watch what we say. Life and death is in the power of the tongue Proverbs 18:21. We have spoken a lot of things that has happened in our life into existence.

We ask God for things and when he give them to us we wonder why it don't work out the way we feel it should. God said He will give us the desires of our heart but our desires might not be his will. You might get what you want but, you might not want what you get.

God is now pouring his spirit unto his people and everyone will not receive him but, to those of us who will he is going to use us like never before. If he gives you a gift, use it. You do not have to kick down the door to be seen because the word of God says that your gift will make room for you. If a door is open for you do not imitate anyone, be who God has called you to be. I am not saying my life now is perfect but we are striving for perfection. We still yet have trials but we give God thanks and high praise through it all. I want to take this time to thank you for reading my book. I thank God every day for everything I have been through, because I came through it. I am not stuck in it.

Pastor Washington after getting out the hospital
from her first decompression surgery

Pastor Washington 295 pounds diagnosis with
toxemia. Blood pressure reached stroke levels

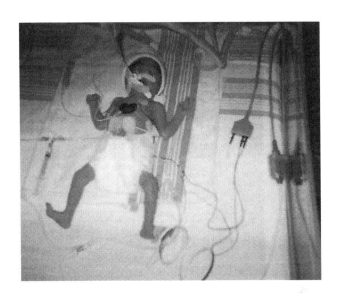

Praise in the (NICU) neonatal intensive care unit. She
was born 27 weeks weighing 2 pounds 6 ounces.

Pastor Washington at first Pastoral anniversary

Made in the USA
Middletown, DE
23 February 2018